KB271439

학습 진도표

본책은 오늘, 워크북은 내일! 부담되지 않은 분량을 정해서 꾸준히 공부하세요.

		학습 분량	학습일
Unit 1	1일차	☐ Mainbook	◯ 월 ◯ 일
Unit 1	2일차	☐ Workbook	◯ 월 ◯ 일
Unit 2	3일차	☐ Main book	◯ 월 ◯ 일
Unit 2	4일차	☐ Workbook	◯ 월 ◯ 일
Unit 3	5일차	☐ Main book	◯ 월 ◯ 일
Unit 3	6일차	☐ Workbook	◯ 월 ◯ 일
Unit 4	7일차	☐ Main book	◯ 월 ◯ 일
Unit 4	8일차	☐ Workbook	◯ 월 ◯ 일
Unit 5	9일차	☐ Main book	◯ 월 ◯ 일
Unit 5	10일차	☐ Workbook	◯ 월 ◯ 일
Unit 6	11일차	☐ Main book	◯ 월 ◯ 일
Unit 6	12일차	☐ Workbook	◯ 월 ◯ 일
Unit 7	13일차	☐ Main book	◯ 월 ◯ 일
Unit 7	14일차	☐ Workbook	◯ 월 ◯ 일
Unit 8	15일차	☐ Main book	◯ 월 ◯ 일
Unit 8	16일차	☐ Workbook	◯ 월 ◯ 일
Unit 9	17일차	☐ Main book	◯ 월 ◯ 일
Unit 9	18일차	☐ Workbook	◯ 월 ◯ 일
Unit 10	19일차	☐ Main book	◯ 월 ◯ 일
Unit 10	20일차	☐ Workbook	◯ 월 ◯ 일

		학습 분량	학습일
Unit 11	21일차	☐ Mainbook	◯ 월 ◯ 일
Unit 11	22일차	☐ Workbook	◯ 월 ◯ 일
Unit 12	23일차	☐ Main book	◯ 월 ◯ 일
Unit 12	24일차	☐ Workbook	◯ 월 ◯ 일
Unit 13	25일차	☐ Main book	◯ 월 ◯ 일
Unit 13	26일차	☐ Workbook	◯ 월 ◯ 일
Unit 14	27일차	☐ Main book	◯ 월 ◯ 일
Unit 14	28일차	☐ Workbook	◯ 월 ◯ 일
Unit 15	29일차	☐ Main book	◯ 월 ◯ 일
Unit 15	30일차	☐ Workbook	◯ 월 ◯ 일
Unit 16	31일차	☐ Main book	◯ 월 ◯ 일
Unit 16	32일차	☐ Workbook	◯ 월 ◯ 일
Unit 17	33일차	☐ Main book	◯ 월 ◯ 일
Unit 17	34일차	☐ Workbook	◯ 월 ◯ 일
Unit 18	35일차	☐ Main book	◯ 월 ◯ 일
Unit 18	36일차	☐ Workbook	◯ 월 ◯ 일
Unit 19	37일차	☐ Main book	◯ 월 ◯ 일
Unit 19	38일차	☐ Workbook	◯ 월 ◯ 일
Unit 20	39일차	☐ Main book	◯ 월 ◯ 일
Unit 20	40일차	☐ Workbook	◯ 월 ◯ 일

기적의 직독직해

120 words B

E2K 지음

기적의 직독직해: 120 words B

Miracle Series – Quick Reading and Understanding

초판 발행 · 2024년 12월 23일

지은이 · E2K
발행인 · 이종원
발행처 · 길벗스쿨
출판사 등록일 · 2006년 7월 1일 | **주소** · 서울시 마포구 월드컵로 10길 56(서교동)
대표 전화 · 02)332-0931 | **팩스** · 02)322-3895
홈페이지 · www.gilbutschool.co.kr | **이메일** · gilbut@gilbut.co.kr

기획 및 책임편집 · 이경희(natura@gilbut.co.kr), 김소이 | **디자인** · 강은경, 신세진 | **제작** · 손일순
영업마케팅 · 문세연, 박선경, 박다슬 | **웹마케팅** · 박달님, 이재윤, 이지수, 나혜연 | **영업관리** · 정경화
독자지원 · 윤정아

전산편집 · 연디자인 | **표지삽화** · 오킹 | **본문삽화** · 천소
인쇄 · 대원문화사 | **제본** · 신정문화사 | **녹음** · 와이알미디어

✽ 잘못 만든 책은 구입한 서점에서 바꿔 드립니다.
✽ 이 책은 저작권법에 따라 보호받는 저작물이므로 무단전재와 무단복제를 금합니다.
　이 책의 전부 또는 일부를 이용하려면 반드시 사전에 저작권자와 길벗스쿨의 서면 동의를 받아야 합니다.

ⒸE2K, 2024
ISBN 979-11-6406-847-0 64740 (길벗 도서번호 30623)
정가 16,000원

독자의 1초를 아껴주는 정성 길벗출판사
길벗 | IT실용서, IT/일반 수험서, IT전문서, 경제실용서, 취미실용서, 건강실용서, 자녀교육서
더퀘스트 | 인문교양서, 비즈니스서
길벗이지톡 | 어학단행본, 어학수험서
길벗스쿨 | 국어학습서, 수학학습서, 유아학습서, 어학학습서, 어린이교양서, 교과서

길벗스쿨 공식 카페 〈기적의 공부방〉 · cafe.naver.com/gilbutschool
인스타그램 / 카카오플러스친구 · @gilbutschool

제 품 명	기적의 직독직해 120B
제조사명	길벗스쿨
제조국명	대한민국
전화번호	02-332-0931
주　소	서울시 마포구 월드컵로 10길 56 (서교동)
제조년월	판권에 별도 표기
사용연령	**10세 이상**

KC마크는 이 제품이 공통안전기준에 적합하였음을 의미합니다.

기적의 직독직해

끊어 읽기를 통한 직독직해 연습은
영어 이해력, 읽기 속도, 정확성을 동시에 키워주는 필수 학습법입니다.

초등 저학년 단계에서는 주로 단어와 문맥을 통해 대략적인 의미를 유추하며 읽었다면, 고학년 시기에는 시험 영어에 대비해 문장을 정확하고 빠르게 이해하며 읽는 능력이 필요합니다. 문장을 의미 단위로 나누어 읽는 '끊어 읽기'를 연습하면 주어, 동사, 목적어 같은 문장 요소들을 자연스럽게 파악할 수 있으며, 길고 복잡한 문장도 더 쉽게 이해할 수 있게 됩니다. 이렇게 하면 문장을 앞뒤로 왔다갔다 하지 않고도 어순 그대로 읽으면서 즉시 이해하는 '직독직해' 실력이 길러집니다.

1 빠르고 정확한 문장 이해를 위한 끊어 읽기 훈련
의미 단위별 끊어 읽기를 통해 문장 전체를 정확히 이해하며 문장 구조를 파악하는 능력을 키웁니다.

2 다양한 장르의 흥미로운 글감을 골고루!
고학년 학생들의 흥미를 유발하는 뉴스와 지식, 전기문, 고전 동화, 창작 스토리 등 다양한 장르를 담았으며, 권당 160~200개의 연관 키워드를 함께 익힐 수 있도록 구성했습니다.

3 직독직해 실력을 높이는 핵심 문법과 문장 구조 알기
〈Grammar Point〉, 〈직독직해 Boost Up!〉 코너를 통해 주요 문법과 핵심 문장 구조를 익히고 실전에 활용할 수 있도록 합니다.

How to Study

Step 1
리딩 지문 읽기

지문 및 단어 듣기

주요 단어와 우리말 뜻을 보여줍니다.

먼저, 지문을 읽습니다. QR코드를 찍어서 원어민 음성을 들으며 눈으로 지문을 쫓아 읽습니다. 이 과정에서 주제와 대략적인 내용을 파악한 다음, 정확한 이해를 위해 문장 하나하나를 자세히 읽어 나갑니다.
낯선 어휘는 오른쪽의 단어 리스트를 통해 의미를 참고합니다.

Step 2
확인 테스트

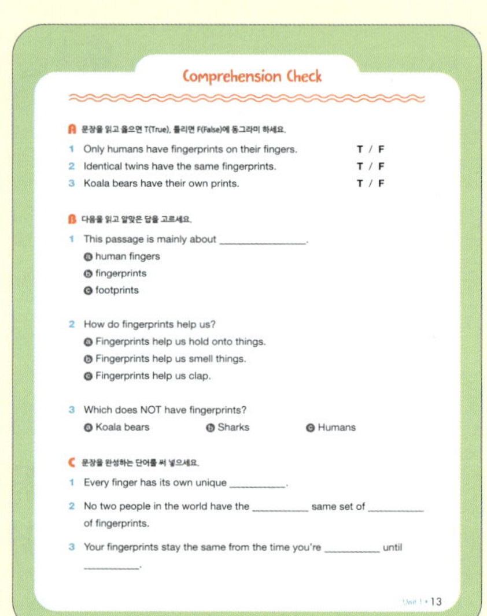

지문 내용을 잘 이해했는지 문제를 통해 확인합니다.
A유형　서술된 문장이 옳은지 그른지를 판단하여 T 또는 F에 동그라미 하기
B유형　지문 내용을 토대로 질문에 알맞은 답을 고르기
C유형　알맞은 단어를 넣어 문장 완성하기

길벗스쿨 e클래스

eclass.gilbut.co.kr
길벗스쿨 e클래스에서 내려 받으세요.

- MP3 바로 듣기 및 전체 다운로드
- 워크시트 5종 다운로드

직독직해 **Boost Up!**

8가지 핵심 문장 구조를 끊어 읽는 보너스 Tip

직독직해를 위해 알아둬야 할 문장 해석법 8가지를 제공합니다. 문장 구조를 이해하여 단어 위치에 따라 어떤 의미로 해석해야 하는지를 익힐 수 있습니다.

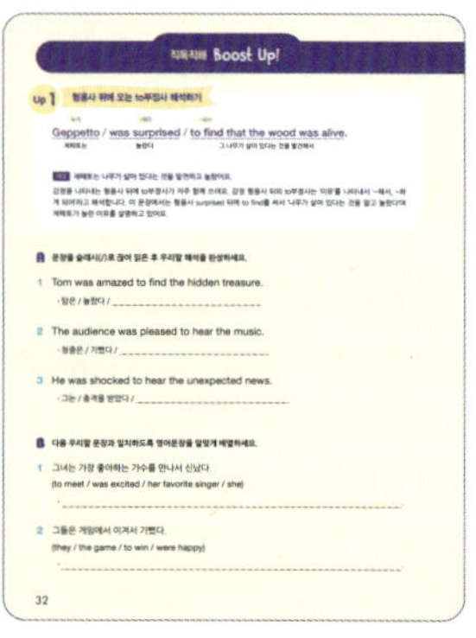

관용어구나 문형에 대한 간략한 설명으로 문장 이해를 돕습니다.

독해가 까다로운 문장에 대해 자세히 해설합니다. 문법과 구조를 이해하여 유사 문장을 해석할 수 있게 합니다.

정확한 문장 독해를 위해, 의미 단위로 단어들을 뭉쳐서 뜻을 파악하는 연습을 합니다.
/(슬래시)로 구분된 영어 어구와 그에 해당하는 우리말 뜻을 확인하며 다시 한 번 지문을 읽어 나갑니다. 빈칸을 채우면서 해석에 주의가 필요한 문장들의 뜻을 제대로 이해했는지 확인합니다.

본책 학습 후 워크북 풀이를 통해 어휘력 보강과 지문 복습을 합니다.
A유형 본책에서 다룬 필수 어휘를 따라 쓰며 뜻 익히기
B유형 우리말 뜻에 알맞은 영단어와 연결하기
C유형 단어 선택 문제를 풀며 지문을 다시 한 번 철저하게 복습하기

부가 학습자료 · 총정리 테스트 · 무료 워크시트 5종

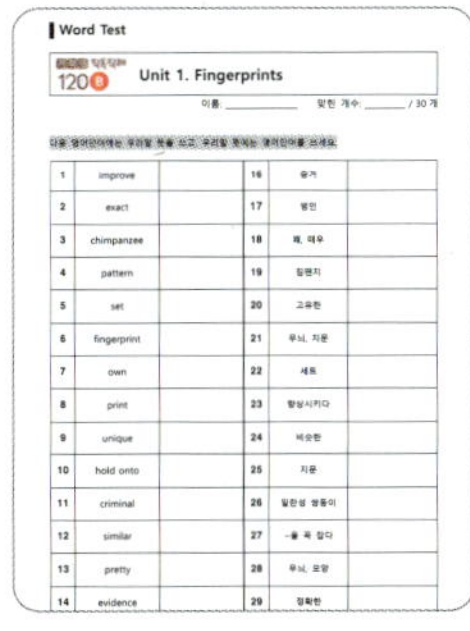

단어 테스트

끊어 읽기 연습

딕테이션

영작 연습

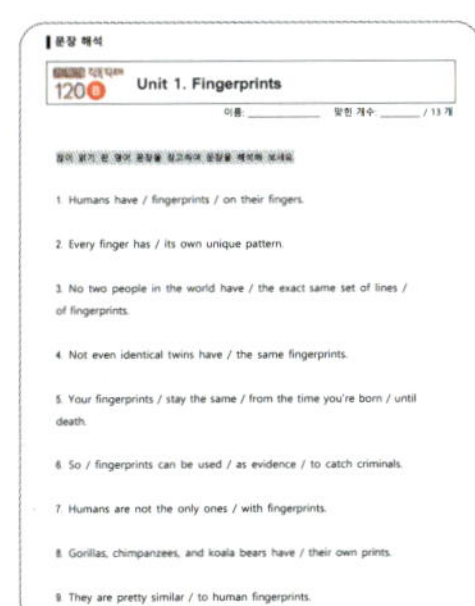

문장 해석

직독직해를 위한 가이드!

우리가 영어를 어렵게 느끼는 가장 큰 이유는 우리말과 영어의 서로 다른 어순 때문일 겁니다. 우리말은 '나는 물을 마신다'라는 어순이지만, 영어는 '나는 마신다 물을'로 우리말과 다른 어순을 갖기 때문이에요. 영어를 우리말 순서에 맞춰 해석하는 것은 좋지 않은 습관입니다. 영어 어순 그대로 읽어가며 바로바로 뜻을 파악하는 영어식 사고에 익숙해져야 해요. 그렇게 되면 리딩 속도가 빨라지는 것은 물론, 더욱 정확하고 완벽한 독해를 해낼 수 있습니다.

영어 어순대로 읽는 즉시 문장의 뜻을 이해하는 것, 즉 직독직해를 할 수 있으려면 단어들을 묶어서 하나의 의미 덩어리로 읽어낼 수 있어야 해요. 일명 '끊어 읽기' 연습을 통해 의미 단위로 구분하여 이해하는 힘을 기를 수 있습니다. 다음에 제시하는 기본 규칙을 적용하여 의미 단위로 끊어 읽는 연습을 해보세요. 많은 글을 읽으며 연습하다 보면 문장을 파악하는 감각이 저절로 생겨날 것입니다.

'주어+동사'를 찾아서 해석해요.

영어 문장은 '누가'(주어)+'행동한다'(동사)를 나타내는 단어들로 시작해요. 어디까지가 '누가'를 나타내고 어디까지 '행동한다'를 의미하는지 파악하는 게 무엇보다 중요합니다. '주어+동사'를 찾아서 한 묶음으로 끊어 이해해 보세요.

예 **The sun rises** / in the east.
　해가　　　　 뜬다

She washes / her hands.
그녀는 씻는다

Dorothy and her dog, Toto, follow / the yellow brick road.
도로시와 그녀의 개 '토토'는　　　　　　 따라간다　　　← 주어가 길어지는 경우도 있어요.

They will be waiting / for you.　　　← 동사구가 여러 단어로 이루어지기도 해요. (미래 진행형)
그들은　기다리고 있을 것이다

The puppet was called / "Pinocchio."　　← 동사구가 여러 단어로 이루어지기도 해요.
그 인형은　　　　 불렸다　　　　　　　　　　(수동태)

'주어+동사' 뒤에 명사가 올 때

'누가 ~한다'라는 말 뒤에는 보통 '무엇을'이란 말이 나옵니다.

예 **Jason ate / an ice cream.**
제이슨은 먹었다   아이스크림을

Birds drink / water / every day.
새는 마신다   물을

be동사 뒤에 오는 '명사'는 신분이나 정체를 나타냅니다. 그래서 '주어+be동사+명사'는 주로
'주어는 (신분이) ~이다'로 이해하면 됩니다.

예 **My mom is / a nurse.**
우리 엄마는 ~이다   간호사

Mozart was / a genius musician.   ⟵ 명사 앞에 명사를 수식하는 말이 들어가기도 해요.
모짜르트는 ~였다   천재 음악가

'주어+동사' 뒤에 형용사가 올 때

주어+동사 뒤에 형용사가 올 때는 주어의 상태가 어떠한지를 말해요. '누가 (기분이) 어떠하다'
또는 '무엇이 (상태가) 어떠하다'라고 해석합니다.

예 **Jane feels / happy.**
제인은 느낀다   행복한   ⟵ 제인은 행복하다

This food smells / bad.
이 음식은 냄새 난다   안 좋은   ⟵ 이 음식은 안 좋은 냄새가 난다

My father is / sick / with the cold.
아빠는 ~이다   아픈   ⟵ 아빠는 아프다

'주어+동사' 뒤에 '전치사+명사'가 올 때

'어디에서'를 나타내는 덩어리들은 보통 '전치사+명사'로 이루어집니다. at, on, in, from 등이 대
표적인 전치사예요.

예 **They danced / on the stage.**
그들은 춤췄다   무대에서

Amy came / from Chicago.
에이미는 왔다　　　시카고에서

Some animals live / in the desert.
몇몇 동물들이 산다　　　　　사막에

'전치사+명사' 덩어리가 '언제'를 나타내기도 합니다.

예 Deserts are cold / at nights.
사막은 춥다　　　　　　밤에

I have a test / on Monday.
나는 시험이 있다　　　월요일에

He gets up early / in the morning.
그는 일찍 일어난다　　　아침에

문장 중간에 'to+동사원형'이 올 때

주어+동사 외에 또 다른 동사가 문장 중간에 등장할 때가 있어요. 'to+동사원형' 형태의 덩어리들은 다양하게 해석될 수 있는데, 맥락에 따라 '~하기 위해서' 또는 '~하는 것', '~할/~하는'으로 해석됩니다.

예 I saved / some money / to help my friend.　　⋯ to: ~하기 위해
나는 저축했다 돈을　　　　　　　내 친구를 돕기 위해

I will go / to the library / to borrow some books.　⋯ to: ~하기 위해
나는 갈 것이다　도서관에　　　　책을 몇 권 빌리러

It is fun / to ride bicycles.　　⋯ to: ~하는 것
재미있다　　자전거를 타는 것은

I need some water / to drink.　　⋯ to: ~할
나는 물이 필요하다　　　마실

'주어+동사' 뒤에 목적어가 두 개 올 때

주어+동사 뒤에 목적어가 두 개 올 때는 '…에게 ~을 한다'라는 의미로 해석하면 됩니다.

예 Mr. Brown teaches / us / English.
브라운 선생님은 가르친다　　　우리에게　영어를

I gave / Jane / a Christmas card / last Sunday.
나는 줬다　제인에게　성탄절 카드를

'주어+동사+목적어' 뒤에 목적어를 보충 설명하는 말이 올 때

주어+동사 뒤에 목적어 하나가 오는 것으로 그치지 않고, 목적어의 상태를 나타내는 단어가 같이 따라올 수 있어요. 이때는 '목적어를 ~하게 만든다/한다'라고 해석합니다.

예 This book made / me / happy.
이 책은 만들었다　　　　　나를　행복하게

They named / their baby / Sam.
그들은 이름붙였다　　　그들의 아기를　　샘이라고

접속사나 쉼표(,)를 기준으로 의미가 나뉠 때

그리고(and), 그러나(but), 왜냐하면(because), ~할 때(when) 등 다양한 의미의 접속사를 중심으로 의미가 나뉩니다. 문장을 읽어가다 내용의 흐름을 바꾸는 이러한 접속사가 나오면 끊어 읽기를 하세요.

예 He came to the party / but she didn't.
그는 파티에 왔다　　　　　　　하지만 그녀는 안 왔다

My mom peeled the potatoes, / and I washed the lettuces.
엄마가 감자를 벗겼다　　　　　　　그리고 나는 상추를 씻었다

Pam is worried / because her cat is ill.
팸은 걱정한다　　　왜냐하면 그녀의 고양이가 아프기 때문이다

문장 앞에 삽입구가 들어갈 때

주어+동사로 시작하기 전에 문장 앞에 삽입구가 오기도 합니다. 삽입구 뒤에 보통 쉼표(,)가 따라오기 때문에 주어+동사와 쉽게 구분할 수 있어요.

예 One day, / I found an old sticker.
어느 날　　　　나는 오래된 스티커를 발견했다

For example, / ants have three body parts.
예를 들면　　　　　개미는 몸통이 세 부분으로 나누어져 있다

Thanks to your help, / I could finish my homework.
너의 도움 덕분에　　　　　　내 숙제를 끝낼 수 있었어

Contents

Fingerprints

Humans have fingerprints on their fingers. Every finger has its own unique pattern. No two people in the world have the exact same set of lines of fingerprints. Not even identical twins have the same fingerprints. Your fingerprints stay the same from the time you're born until death. So fingerprints can be used as evidence to catch criminals.

Humans are not the only ones with fingerprints. Gorillas, chimpanzees, and koala bears have their own prints. They are pretty similar to human fingerprints.

So why do we have fingerprints? Fingerprints make the ends of our fingers rough. This improves our sense of touch. Also, rough skin helps us hold onto things.

- **fingerprint** 지문
- **own** 고유한
- **unique** 독특한
- **pattern** 무늬, 모양
- **exact** 정확한
- **set** 세트
- **identical twins** 일란성 쌍둥이
- **evidence** 증거
- **criminal** 범인
- **chimpanzee** 침팬지
- **print** 무늬, 지문
- **pretty** 꽤, 매우
- **similar** 비슷한
- **improve** 향상시키다
- **hold onto** ~을 꼭 잡다

Comprehension Check

A 문장을 읽고 옳으면 T(True), 틀리면 F(False)에 동그라미 하세요.

1 Only humans have fingerprints on their fingers.　　**T / F**

2 Identical twins have the same fingerprints.　　**T / F**

3 Koala bears have their own prints.　　**T / F**

B 다음을 읽고 알맞은 답을 고르세요.

1 This passage is mainly about ________________.

   ⓐ human fingers

   ⓑ fingerprints

   ⓒ footprints

2 How do fingerprints help us?

   ⓐ Fingerprints help us hold onto things.

   ⓑ Fingerprints help us smell things.

   ⓒ Fingerprints help us clap.

3 Which does NOT have fingerprints?

   ⓐ Koala bears　　　　ⓑ Sharks　　　　ⓒ Humans

C 문장을 완성하는 단어를 써 넣으세요.

1 Every finger has its own unique __________.

2 No two people in the world have the __________ same set of __________ of fingerprints.

3 Your fingerprints stay the same from the time you're __________ until __________.

Read and Understand

● 잘 읽고 이해했나요? 문장의 정확한 의미를 알아보세요.

1. Humans have / fingerprints / on their fingers.
사람들은 가지고 있다　　지문을　　________________

2. Every finger has / its own unique pattern.
모든 손가락은 가지고 있다　　________________

→ no two people는 '어떤 두 사람도 ~하지 않다'라고 해석해요.

3. No two people in the world have / the exact same set of lines /
________________　정확히 같은 선 세트를

of fingerprints.
지문의

→ not even은 '심지어 ~도 ~않다'라는 뜻이에요.

4. Not even identical twins have / the same fingerprints.
________________　똑같은 지문을

5. Your fingerprints stay the same / from the time you're born / until death.
________________　여러분이 태어날 때부터　　죽을 때까지

→ 여기서 as는 '~로, ~로서'라는 뜻이에요.

6. So / fingerprints can be used / as evidence / to catch criminals.
그래서 지문은 사용될 수 있다　　증거로　　________________

7. Humans are not the only ones / with fingerprints.
사람들이 유일한 종은 아니다　　________________

8. Gorillas, chimpanzees, and koala bears / have their own prints.
고릴라, 침팬지, 그리고 코알라는　　________________

pretty는 '꽤, 매우'라는 뜻의 부사로도 쓰여요.
→ similar to는 '~과 비슷한'이라는 뜻이에요.

9. They are pretty similar / to human fingerprints.
________________　인간의 지문들과

10. So / why do we have / fingerprints?
그러면 ________________　지문을

14

11. Fingerprints make / the ends of our fingers / rough.

지문들은 만든다   거칠게

12. This improves / our sense of touch.

이것은 향상시킨다

13. Also, / rough skin helps / us hold onto things.

또한   거친 피부는 도와준다

Grammar Point — Not으로 시작하는 문장

본문 쏙 Not even identical twins have the same fingerprints.
심지어 일란성 쌍둥이도 똑같은 지문을 갖고 있지 않다.

이 문장은 Even identical twins don't have the same fingerprints.에서 not을 맨 앞으로 뺀 형태입니다. 이렇게 not을 문장의 맨 앞에 넣는 이유는 '아니다'라는 부정의 의미를 강조하기 위해서랍니다.

확인문제 **1** Not even my teacher knows the result.

2 Not even Jane remembered my name.

A New Life in America

The Kims immigrated to the United States from South Korea. Ms. Kim made *tteok* to give to her new neighbors. Mr. Kim, Ms. Kim, Jongmin, and Minhee rang their next-door neighbor's doorbell. Mr. Randy and his family greeted them at the door and welcomed them inside.

The Kims tried to take off their shoes, but Mr. Randy said that it was okay to wear shoes in his house. It was a surprising experience for the Kims.

The Kims gave *tteok*, a traditional Korean food that is made of rice and beans, to the Randys. Ms. Kim explained that Koreans give *tteok* to their new neighbors when they move. Ms. Randy thanked her and invited them into the kitchen for some homemade apple pie. It was a great cultural exchange.

- **immigrate** 이민을 오다
- **United States** 미국
- **South Korea** 한국
- **neighbor** 이웃
- **rang** (초인종을) 눌렀다 (ring (초인종을) 누르다)
- **next-door** 옆집의
- **doorbell** 초인종
- **greet** 인사하다
- **welcome** 환영하다
- **take off** 벗다
- **surprising** 놀라운
- **experience** 경험
- **traditional** 전통적인
- **Korean** 한국의; 한국인
- **rice** 쌀
- **explain** 설명하다
- **homemade** 집에서 만든
- **cultural** 문화의
- **exchange** 교류

Comprehension Check

A 문장을 읽고 옳으면 T(True), 틀리면 F(False)에 동그라미 하세요.

1 The Kims moved to South Korea from the United States.   **T / F**

2 The Kims visited Mr. Randy's house.   **T / F**

3 Ms. Randy gave the Kims some apple pie.   **T / F**

B 다음을 읽고 알맞은 답을 고르세요.

1 This passage is mainly about _________________.

   ⓐ Mr. Randy's house

   ⓑ The Kims' new life in the United States

   ⓒ American traditions

2 Why did the Kims give *tteok* to Mr. Randy and his family?

   ⓐ Because it's a tradition for Koreans to give tteok to their neighbors when they move.

   ⓑ Because the Kims wanted to give them a surprise present.

   ⓒ Because Mr. Randy and his family invited the Kims to a birthday party.

3 What is *tteok*?

   ⓐ It's a traditional Korean food that is made of apple pie.

   ⓑ It's a traditional Korean food that is made of rice and beans.

   ⓒ It's a traditional Korean food that is made of bread and cream.

C 문장을 완성하는 단어를 써 넣으세요.

1 The Kims __________ to the United States from South Korea.

2 The Kims tried to __________ __________ their shoes.

3 It was a great cultural __________.

● 잘 읽고 이해했나요? 문장의 정확한 의미를 알아보세요.

→ the Kims는 '김씨네 가족'을 뜻해요.

1. The Kims immigrated / to the United States / from South Korea.
__________________________　　미국으로　　　　　　　한국에서

2. Ms. Kim made / *tteok* / to give to her new neighbors.
김씨 아주머니는 만들었다　떡을　　__________________________

→ ring은 종을 '울리다'뿐만 아니라 초인종을 '누르다'라는 뜻으로도 쓰여요. ←

3. Mr. Kim, Ms. Kim, Jongmin, and Minhee / rang their next-door
김씨 아저씨, 김씨 아주머니, 종민, 그리고 민희는　　　　　　　__________________

neighbor's doorbell.
____

4. Mr. Randy and his family / greeted them / at the door /
랜디씨와 그의 가족은　　　　　　　그들에게 인사했고　　문 앞에서

and welcomed them inside.
____

→ try to는 '~하려고 하다/노력하다'라는 뜻이에요.

5. The Kims / tried to take off their shoes, / but Mr. Randy said /
김씨네 가족은　__________________________　하지만 랜디씨가 말했다

→ it은 가주어이고 to 이하가 진주어예요.

that it was okay / to wear shoes / in his house.
괜찮다고　　　　　신발을 신는 것은　　그의 집에서

6. It was / a surprising experience / for the Kims.
그것은 ~였다　__________________________　김씨네 가족에게

→ 여기서 Korean은 '한국의'라는 뜻의 형용사예요.

7. The Kims gave *tteok*, / a traditional Korean food / that is made of rice
김씨네 가족은 떡을 주었다　　　　__________________________　쌀과 팥으로 만들어진

and beans, / to the Randys.
랜디씨 가족에게

→ 여기서 Korean은 '한국인'이라는 뜻의 명사예요.

8. Ms. Kim explained / that Koreans give *tteok* / to their new neighbors /
김씨 아주머니는 설명했다　　　한국인들은 떡을 준다고　　　　그들의 새로운 이웃들에게

when they move.

____

9. Ms. Randy thanked her / and invited them / into the kitchen /
_______________________ 그리고 그들을 안내했다　　　　　부엌으로

for some homemade apple pie.
집에서 만든 애플파이를 주기 위해

10. It was / a great cultural exchange.
그것은 ~였다 _______________________

Grammar Point — 명사를 뒤에서 꾸며주는 **that**절

본문 쏙 The Kims gave *tteok*, a traditional Korean food <u>that</u> is made of rice and beans, to the Randys.
김씨네 가족은 쌀과 팥으로 만든 한국의 전통 음식인 떡을 랜디씨 가족에게 줬다.

여기서 that은 앞에 나온 명사 food를 보충 설명하기 위해 쓰였어요. 따라서 밑줄 친 that절이 food를 꾸며주는 것이므로 food ~ beans를 '쌀과 팥으로 만들어진 음식'이라고 해석하면 됩니다. 이런 용도로 쓰이는 that을 '관계대명사'라고 하고, 이렇게 사물을 꾸며줄 때는 which로 바꿔 써도 돼요.

확인문제 1 It is a robot that is made with blocks.

____

2 This is the book that changed my life.

____

Pocahontas

Pocahontas is one of the most famous women in Native American history. There is a famous story about Pocahontas saving John Smith's life.

Pocahontas was the daughter of the chief of the Powhatan people. They were Native Americans. When Pocahontas was about twelve years old, strange Englishmen came to the Powhatans. They wanted to take their land, so the Powhatans and the Englishmen fought.

One day, the leader of the Englishmen, John Smith, was caught and the chief of the Powhatans was about to kill him. Pocahontas begged her father not to kill the man and she rescued him. She wanted both of them to live in peace and harmony. Pocahontas played an important role between the Native Americans and the Englishmen.

- **women** 여자들 (woman 여자)
- **history** 역사
- **chief** 추장, 족장
- **strange** 낯선, 이상한
- **Englishmen** 영국인들 (Englishman 영국인)
- **leader** 지도자, 대표
- **be about to** 막 ~하려 하다
- **beg** 간청하다
- **rescue** 구하다
- **peace** 평화
- **harmony** 조화
- **play a role** 역할을 하다

Comprehension Check

A 문장을 읽고 옳으면 T(True), 틀리면 F(False)에 동그라미 하세요.

1 The Powhatan people were Native Americans. **T / F**

2 Pocahontas was the daughter of the chief of the Powhatan people. **T / F**

3 Pocahontas rescued the leader of the Powhatans. **T / F**

B 다음을 읽고 알맞은 답을 고르세요.

1 This passage is mainly about _________________.
   ⓐ Pocahontas   ⓑ the Englishmen   ⓒ the Powhatans

2 Why did the chief of the Powhatans want to kill John Smith?
   ⓐ Because John Smith wanted to marry Pocahontas.
   ⓑ Because Native Americans wanted to move to England.
   ⓒ Because Englishmen wanted to take their land.

3 Who rescued John Smith?
   ⓐ The leader of the Englishmen
   ⓑ Pocahontas
   ⓒ Native Americans

C 문장을 완성하는 단어를 써 넣으세요.

1 Pocahontas is one of the most famous __________ in Native American history.

2 There is a __________ story about Pocahontas saving John Smith's __________.

3 When Pocahontas was about __________ years old, __________ Englishmen came to the Powhatans.

● 잘 읽고 이해했나요? 문장의 정확한 의미를 알아보세요.

→ famous(유명한)의 최상급은 most famous(가장 유명한)예요.

1. Pocahontas is / one of the most famous women / in Native American
포카혼타스는 ~이다 　　　　　　　　　　　　　　　　　　　　 미국 원주민 역사에서

history.

2. There is a famous story / about Pocahontas / saving John Smith's life.
유명한 이야기가 있다 　　　　　　 포카혼타스에 대한

3. Pocahontas was / the daughter of the chief / of the Powhatan people.
포카혼타스는 ~였다 　　　　　　　　　　　　　　　　　　 포와탄 부족의

↳ Native American은 북미 지역에서 원래부터 살고 있었던 원주민들(인디언)을 뜻해요.

4. They were / Native Americans.
그들은 ~였다

← Englishman(영국인)의 복수형은 Englishmen이에요.

5. When Pocahontas was / about twelve years old, / strange Englishmen /
포카혼타스가 ~였을 때 　　　　　　 12살 쯤

came to the Powhatans.
포와탄 부족에게 왔다

6. They wanted / to take their land, / so the Powhatans and the
그들은 원했다 　　　　　　　　　　　　　　 그래서 포와탄 부족과 영국인들은

Englishmen / fought.
싸웠다

← was caught는 수동태로서 '잡혔다'라는 뜻이에요.

7. One day, / the leader of the Englishmen, John Smith, / was caught /
어느 날 　　　 영국인들의 지도자인 존 스미스가 　　　　　　　　　　　 잡혔다

and the chief of the Powhatans / was about to kill him.
그리고 포와탄의 추장이

8. Pocahontas begged / her father / not to kill the man /
포카혼타스는 간청했다 　　　 그녀의 아버지에게

and she rescued him.
그래서 그녀는 그를 구했다

9. She wanted / both of them / to live in peace and harmony.
그녀는 원했다　　　그들 양쪽 모두가

10. Pocahontas played an important role / between / the Native Americans
사이에서　　　미국 원주민들과 영국인들

and the Englishmen.

Grammar Point one of + 최상급 + 복수명사

본문 쏙 Pocahontas is one of the most famous women in Native American history.

포카혼타스는 미국 원주민 역사에서 가장 유명한 여성들 중 한 명이다.

one of my friends(내 친구들 중 한 명), one of the problems(문제들 중 하나)와 같이 〈one of+복수명사〉는 '~들 중 하나'라는 뜻이에요. 그런데 최상급이 추가되어 〈one of+최상급+복수명사〉 형태가 되면 '가장 ~한 ~들 중 하나'라는 뜻이 돼요. 따라서 색자 부분은 '가장 유명한 여성들 중 한 명'이라고 해석하면 됩니다.

확인문제 **1** He is one of the richest people in the world.

2 Baseball is one of the most popular sports in Korea.

Pinocchio

Once upon a time, a carpenter found a talking piece of wood and he gave it to his friend, Geppetto. Geppetto wanted to make a puppet, so he took it home. He would call the puppet Pinocchio.

When he started to carve the wood, a voice squealed. "Ouch! That hurt!" Geppetto was surprised to find that the wood was alive. He carved a head, hair, eyes, and a nose. When he carved out the nose, it grew longer and longer. Geppetto cut it down, but it remained a long nose.

When Geppetto was almost finished making Pinocchio, it took Geppetto's wig off and ran away from the house. "You naughty boy! Come back!" Geppetto screamed, but Pinocchio couldn't hear because Geppetto had forgotten to carve the ears.

- **carpenter** 목수
- **puppet** 꼭두각시 인형
- **carve** 조각하다
- **squeal** 꽥 소리를 지르다
- **surprised** 놀란
- **alive** 살아 있는
- **grew** 자랐다 (grow 자라다)
- **remain** 계속[여전히] ~이다
- **finish** 끝내다
- **wig** 가발
- **naughty** 버릇없는, 개구쟁이의
- **scream** 소리를 [비명을] 지르다
- **forgotten** forget(잊어버리다)의 과거분사

Comprehension Check

A 문장을 읽고 옳으면 T(True), 틀리면 F(False)에 동그라미 하세요.

1 The strange piece of wood could talk.   **T / F**

2 Geppetto wanted to make a naughty boy.   **T / F**

3 When Geppetto carved out the ears, they grew longer and longer. **T / F**

B 다음을 읽고 알맞은 답을 고르세요.

1 This passage is mainly about ______________________.

   a a talking wooden puppet

   b a carpenter

   c Pinocchio's long nose

2 What did Geppetto want to make?

   a A puppet   **b** A toy robot   **c** A chair

3 Why could Pinocchio NOT hear?

   a Because Pinocchio hurt his ears.

   b Because Pinocchio's ears grew longer.

   c Because Geppetto forgot to carve the ears.

C 문장을 완성하는 단어를 써 넣으세요.

1 Once upon a time, a carpenter found a talking piece of __________.

2 When he started to __________ the wood, a voice squealed.

3 Pinocchio took Geppetto's __________ off and ran __________ from the house.

Read and Understand

● 잘 읽고 이해했나요? 문장의 정확한 의미를 알아보세요.

→ 이야기 시작 부분에서 자주 나오는 once upon a time은 '옛날 옛적에, 옛날에'라고 해석하면 돼요.

1. Once upon a time, / a carpenter found / a talking piece of wood /
옛날에　　　　　　　　한 목수가 발견했다

and he gave it / to his friend, Geppetto.
그리고 그는 그것을 줬다　　그의 친구 제페토에게

2. Geppetto wanted / to make a puppet, / so he took it / home.
제페토는 원했다　　　　　　　　　　　　　그래서 그는 그것을 가져갔다　집으로

→ 〈call A B〉는 'A를 B라고 부르다'라는 뜻이에요.

3. He would call / the puppet Pinocchio.
그는 부르려고 했다

→ squeal은 높고 길게 '꽤액, 꺄악' 소리 내는 것을 말해요.

4. When he started / to carve the wood, / a voice squealed.
그가 시작했을 때　　　　　　　　　　　　어떤 목소리가 꽤액 소리를 질렀다

→ be surprised to는 '~해서 놀라다'라는 뜻이에요.

5. "Ouch! That hurt!" / Geppetto was surprised / to find that the wood
아야! 아파요!　　　　　제페토는 놀랐다

was alive.

6. He carved / a head, hair, eyes, and a nose.
그는 조각했다　　머리, 머리카락, 눈, 그리고 코를

→ grow 뒤에 비교급이 나오면 '점점 더 ~해지다'라는 뜻이에요.

7. When he carved out / the nose, / it grew longer and longer.
그가 다 조각했을 때　　　　　코를

8. Geppetto cut it down, / but it remained / a long nose.
그러나 그것은 계속 ~였다　　긴 코

→ finish 뒤에 동사가 목적어로 올 때는 making처럼 동명사 형태를 써야 해요.

9. When Geppetto was almost finished / making Pinocchio, /
제페토가 거의 끝냈을 때　　　　　　　　　　피노키오 만드는 것을

→ took off는 take off(벗다, 벗기다)의 과거형이에요.

it took Geppetto's wig off / and ran away from the house.
그것은 제페토의 가발을 벗겼다

10. "You naughty boy! / Come back!" Geppetto screamed, /
이 버릇없는 놈　　　　돌아와　　　　제페토가 소리를 질렀다

but Pinocchio couldn't hear / because Geppetto had forgotten /
그러나 피노키오는 들을 수가 없었다

to carve the ears.
귀를 조각하는 것을

제페토가 소리를 지른 것보다 귀를 조각하는 것을 깜빡한 것이 먼저 일어난 일이기 때문에, 과거완료인 had forgotten을 쓴 거예요.

본문 쏙 Once upon a time, a carpenter found a **talking** <u>piece of wood</u>.
옛날에 한 목수가 말하는 나무 토막을 발견했다.

명사인 a piece of wood(나무 토막)를 현재분사인 talking(말하는)이 꾸며주고 있어요. 그래서 a talking piece of wood는 '말하는 나무 토막'이라고 해석해요. 이렇게 현재분사는 명사를 꾸며주는 역할도 하는데, 이때는 '~하는'이나 '~하고 있는'이라고 해석하면 됩니다.

확인문제 **1** The running man is my uncle.

2 I want to buy a flying robot.

Flower Scents

When most people think of flowers, they think of sweet scents. But this is not always the case. Not all flowers smell sweet. In fact, some flowers stink. A huge flower in Sumatra, the titan arum, smells like rotten flesh. This smell attracts flies so that the flower can be pollinated.

Why do flowers have scents? There should be a reason. Flowers make chemicals to attract insects or birds. They will visit and pollinate flowers.

Flowers have different smells because they attract different pollinators. Flowers pollinated by bees and butterflies have sweet scents. Flowers pollinated by moths have stronger scents at night than during the day. Flowers pollinated by bats have musty odors. Flowers pollinated by beetles have fruity scents.

- **scent** 향기
- **case** 경우
- **in fact** 사실은
- **stink** 악취가 나다
- **rotten** 썩은
- **flesh** 고기, 살
- **attract** 유인하다
- **pollinate** 수분하다
- **chemical** 화학 물질
- **insect** 곤충
- **pollinator** 꽃가루 매개체
- **musty** 퀴퀴한 냄새가 나는
- **odor** 악취
- **fruity** 과일 향이 강한

Comprehension Check

A 문장을 읽고 옳으면 T(True), 틀리면 F(False)에 동그라미 하세요.

1 Some flowers smell very bad.　　　　　　　　　　　　　　　**T / F**

2 The titan arum attracts flies so that it can be pollinated.　**T / F**

3 Flowers make chemicals that attract people.　　　　　　　　**T / F**

B 다음을 읽고 알맞은 답을 고르세요.

1 This passage is mainly about ________________.

  ⓐ flower sizes

  ⓑ flower shapes

  ⓒ flower scents

2 Which flowers have musty odors?

  ⓐ Flowers pollinated by bats

  ⓑ Flowers pollinated by birds

  ⓒ Flowers pollinated by bees

3 According to the article, what is true?

  ⓐ All flowers smell sweet.

  ⓑ Only birds can pollinate flowers.

  ⓒ The titan arum can be pollinated by flies.

C 문장을 완성하는 단어를 써 넣으세요.

1 Not all flowers smell sweet. In __________, some flowers __________.

2 The titan arum smells like __________ flesh.

3 Flowers pollinated by __________ have stronger scents at night than during the day.

● 잘 읽고 이해했나요? 문장의 정확한 의미를 알아보세요.

think of는 '~을 생각하다, 떠올리다'라는 뜻이에요.

1. When most people think of flowers, / they think of sweet scents.
대부분의 사람들은 꽃을 생각할 때

2. But / this is not always the case.
하지만

3. Not all flowers / smell sweet.
모든 꽃들이 ~하지는 않는다

4. In fact, / some flowers stink.
사실

smell like는 '~같은 냄새가 나다' 라는 뜻이에요.

5. A huge flower in Sumatra, / the titan arum, / smells like rotten flesh.
수마트라에 있는 거대한 꽃인   타이탄 아룸은

so that은 '~하기 위해서', '~하도록'이라는 뜻으로 목적을 나타내요.

6. This smell attracts flies / so that the flower can be pollinated.
꽃이 수분될 수 있도록

7. Why / do flowers have / scents?   There should be a reason.
왜   꽃들은 가지고 있을까?   향기를   이유가 있을 것이다

8. Flowers make / chemicals / to attract insects or birds.
꽃들은 만든다   화학 물질들을

9. They will visit / and pollinate flowers.
그들은 방문할 것이다

10. Flowers have / different smells / because / they attract /
꽃들은 가지고 있다   다른 냄새를   왜냐하면   그들은 유인한다

different pollinators.

11. Flowers / pollinated by bees and butterflies / have sweet scents.
꽃들은 　　　벌과 나비에 의해 수분되는 　　　　　　　　　　　_______________

12. Flowers / pollinated by moths / have stronger scents / at night /
꽃들은 　_____________________ 　더 강한 향기가 난다 　　　밤에

than during the day.
낮보다

13. Flowers / pollinated by bats / have musty odors.
꽃들은 　　　박쥐에 의해 수분되는 　　　_________________

14. Flowers / pollinated by beetles / have fruity scents.
꽃들은 　_____________________ 　과일 향이 난다

Grammar Point | 명사를 뒤에서 꾸며주는 과거분사구

본문 쏙 Flowers pollinated by bees and butterflies have sweet scents.
벌과 나비에 의해 수분되는 꽃들은 달콤한 향기가 난다.

과거분사구인 pollinated by bees and butterflies(벌과 나비에 의해 수분되는)가 명사인 flowers(꽃들)를 뒤에서 꾸며주고 있어요. 그래서 '벌들과 나비들에 의해 수분되는 꽃들'이라고 해석하면 돼요. 이렇게 과거분사가 '구'를 이루어 길어지면 명사를 뒤에서 꾸며준답니다.

확인문제 **1** A boy named Peter wrote the story.

2 Look at the cake covered with chocolate!

Up 1 형용사 뒤에 오는 to부정사 해석하기

누가   ~하다   ~해서

Geppetto / was surprised / to find that the wood was alive.

제페토는   놀랐다   그 나무가 살아 있다는 것을 발견해서

해설 제페토는 나무가 살아 있다는 것을 발견하고 놀랐어요.

감정을 나타내는 형용사 뒤에 to부정사가 자주 함께 쓰여요. 감정 형용사 뒤의 to부정사는 '이유'를 나타내서 '~해서, ~하게 되어'라고 해석합니다. 이 문장에서는 형용사 surprised 뒤에 to find를 써서 '나무가 살아 있다는 것을 알고 놀랐다'며 제페토가 놀란 이유를 설명하고 있어요.

🔵 문장을 슬래시(/)로 끊어 읽은 후 우리말 해석을 완성하세요.

1 Tom was amazed to find the hidden treasure.

→ 탐은 / 놀랐다 / ________________________________

2 The audience was pleased to hear the music.

→ 청중은 / 기뻤다 / ________________________________

3 He was shocked to hear the unexpected news.

→ 그는 / 충격을 받았다 / ________________________________

🔵 다음 우리말 문장과 일치하도록 영어문장을 알맞게 배열하세요.

1 그녀는 가장 좋아하는 가수를 만나서 신났다.

(to meet / was excited / her favorite singer / she)

→ ____.

2 그들은 게임에서 이겨서 기뻤다.

(they / the game / to win / were happy)

→ ____.

이렇게 끊어 읽으면 직독직해가 술술!

Up 2 목적을 나타내는 so that 구문 해석하기

누가　　　　한다　　　무엇을　　　~하도록

This smell / attracts / flies / so that the flowers can be pollinated.
이 냄새는　　　　유인한다　　파리를　　　　　　　　꽃이 수분될 수 있도록

해설 **꽃이 수분될 수 있도록 이 냄새는 파리를 유인해요.**

'주어+동사+목적어' 구조의 3형식 문장에 so that 부사절이 따라 붙은 문장입니다. so that은 '~하기 위해서'로 해석하여, so that 뒤에 오는 문장은 앞의 문장의 이유나 목적을 나타냅니다. 이 문장에서 파리를 유인한 이유는 파리가 꽃에 와서 '꽃이 수분될 수 있도록' 하는 것임을 설명합니다.

🅐 문장을 슬래시(/)로 끊어 읽은 후 우리말 해석을 완성하세요.

1 I worked hard so that I could finish my homework.

→ 나는 / 열심히 했다 / ________________________________

2 He eats vegetables so that he stays healthy.

→ 그는 / 채소를 먹는다 / ________________________________

3 We cleaned the table so that it was ready for dinner.

→ 우리는 / 식탁을 닦았다 / ________________________________

🅑 다음 우리말 문장과 일치하도록 영어문장을 알맞게 배열하세요.

1 그녀는 제시간에 일어나기 위해 알람을 맞춘다.

(on time / she / so that / she wakes up / sets an alarm)

→ ____.

2 나는 소포가 일찍 도착하도록 어제 소포를 보냈어요.

(it would arrive / I / early / so that / sent the package / yeaterday)

→ ____.

Exploring a Cave

Today our class went on a field trip to explore a cave. We were all excited and nervous about going into the cave.

When we entered the cave, we saw moss growing on stones and some spider webs. When we passed some white snails crawling on the moss, something hopped in front of us. All the students screamed. It was just a frog. We didn't know that frogs lived in caves.

We kept walking deeper into the cave. There was some movement on the wall. The teacher shone the flashlight and we saw lizards. Then on the ceiling we saw bats folding their wings. Finally, we saw a crayfish in a pool of water in the cave. We didn't know that so many different animals lived in caves.

- **field trip** 체험학습
- **explore** 탐험하다
- **excited** 신이 난
- **nervous** 긴장한
- **enter** 들어가다
- **moss** 이끼
- **snail** 달팽이
- **crawl** 기어가다
- **hop** 팔짝 뛰다
- **in front of** ~앞에
- **deeper** 더 깊이
- **shone** 비췄다
  (**shine** 비추다)
- **flashlight** 손전등
- **ceiling** 천장
- **crayfish** 가재
- **pool** 웅덩이

A 문장을 읽고 옳으면 T(True), 틀리면 F(False)에 동그라미 하세요.

1 The students learned about the cave in their classroom. **T / F**

2 The students saw moss and some spider webs in the cave. **T / F**

3 There were lizards moving on the wall. **T / F**

B 다음을 읽고 알맞은 답을 고르세요.

1 This passage is mainly about _______________.
   ⓐ the school kids
   ⓑ the moss
   ⓒ the cave

2 How did the students feel about going into the cave?
   ⓐ Happy and comfortable
   ⓑ Sad and lonely
   ⓒ Excited and nervous

3 Which animal did the students NOT see in the cave?
   ⓐ White snails
   ⓑ Iguanas
   ⓒ Crayfish

C 문장을 완성하는 단어를 써 넣으세요.

1 Today our class went on a field trip to __________ a cave.

2 We kept walking __________ into the cave.

3 We didn't know that so many __________ animals lived in __________.

● 잘 읽고 이해했나요? 문장의 정확한 의미를 알아보세요.

→ go on a field trip은 '체험학습을 가다'라는 뜻이에요.

1. Today / our class went on a field trip / to explore a cave.
오늘　　　우리 반은 체험학습을 갔다

2. We were all excited / and nervous / about going into the cave.
　　　　　　그리고 긴장이 됐다　　동굴에 들어가는 것에 대해

growing on stones가 moss를 꾸며주고 있어요.

3. When we entered / the cave, / we saw moss / growing on stones /
우리가 들어갔을 때　　　동굴에　　　우리는 이끼를 봤다

and some spider webs.
그리고 약간의 거미줄들을

→ crawling on the moss가 snails를 꾸며주고 있어요.

4. When we passed / some white snails / crawling on the moss, /
우리가 지나갈 때　　　하얀 달팽이 몇 마리를

something hopped / in front of us.
뭔가가 팔짝 뛰어올랐다　　　우리 앞에서

5. All the students / screamed.   It was just a frog.
　　　　　　　　소리를 질렀다　　그것은 단지 개구리였다

6. We didn't know / that frogs lived in caves.
　　　　　　　개구리들이 동굴에 산다는 것을

〈keep + -ing〉는 '계속 ~하다'라는 뜻이에요.

7. We kept walking / deeper into the cave.
　　　　　　　동굴 속으로 더 깊이

8. There was / some movement / on the wall.
있었다　　　어떤 움직임이

9. The teacher shone the flashlight / and we saw lizards.
　　　　　　　　　　　그리고 우리는 도마뱀들을 보았다

10. Then / on the ceiling / we saw bats / folding their wings.
그런 다음　천장 위에서　　　　　우리는 박쥐들을 보았다　________________

11. Finally, / we saw a crayfish / in a pool of water / in the cave.
마지막으로　　우리는 가재를 보았다　________________　동굴 안에 있는

12. We didn't know / that so many different animals lived / in caves.
우리는 몰랐다　________________　동굴에서

Grammar Point　명사를 뒤에서 꾸며주는 현재분사구

본문 쏙 When we entered the cave, we saw moss growing on stones and some spider webs.
우리는 동굴에 들어갔을 때 돌 위에서 자라고 있는 이끼와 거미줄들을 보았다.

현재분사구인 growing on stones(돌 위에서 자라고 있는)가 명사인 moss(이끼)를 뒤에서 꾸며주고 있어요. 그래서 moss~stones를 '돌 위에서 자라고 있는 이끼'라고 해석하면 돼요. 현재분사는 주로 명사를 앞에서 꾸며주지만, 이렇게 '구'를 이루어 길어지면 명사를 뒤에서 꾸며준답니다.

확인문제 **1** I saw a girl dancing on the stage.

2 Look at the bear walking like a human being.

Reduce, Reuse, and Recycle

It's time to learn the three R's of the environment: reduce, reuse, and recycle. Every year, Americans throw away 27 billion glass bottles, 35 million tons of food, and 65 million plastic and metal cans. Where does all of this waste go? It all remains in the land and takes from 100 to 4,000 years to decompose.

The best way to help the environment is to reduce the amount of waste we produce. We should buy products that don't have a lot of packaging. Another way to help the environment is to reuse things instead of throwing them away. Lastly, recycle things to create new products out of the materials from the old ones. We should also look for products that contain recycled materials.

- **environment** 환경
- **reduce** 줄이다
- **reuse** 재사용하다
- **recycle** 재활용하다
- **throw away** 버리다
- **glass** 유리
- **bottle** 병
- **million** 100만
- **decompose** 분해되다
- **amount** 양
- **product** 제품
- **packaging** 포장(재)
- **lastly** 마지막으로
- **look for** 찾다, 구하다

Comprehension Check

A 문장을 읽고 옳으면 T(True), 틀리면 F(False)에 동그라미 하세요.

1 The three R's are reduce, reuse, and return. **T / F**

2 We should buy products that don't have a lot of packaging. **T / F**

3 The best way to help the environment is to recycle. **T / F**

B 다음을 읽고 알맞은 답을 고르세요.

1 This passage is mainly about ________________.

   ⓐ packaging   **ⓑ** the three R's   **ⓒ** food waste

2 How many years does it take to decompose the wastes?

   ⓐ About 1 to 50 years

   ⓑ About 100 to 4,000 years

   ⓒ More than 5,000 years

3 What is the best way to help the environment?

   ⓐ Buying products which have a lot of packaging.

   ⓑ Throwing away products after using them.

   ⓒ Reducing the amount of waste we produce.

C 문장을 완성하는 단어를 써 넣으세요.

1 It's time to learn the three R's of the __________.

2 We should buy products that don't have a lot of __________.

3 Recycle things to create __________ products out of the materials from the __________ ones.

● 잘 읽고 이해했나요? 문장의 정확한 의미를 알아보세요.

→ It's time to...는 '~할 시간이다'라는 뜻이에요.

1. It's time to learn / the three R's of the environment: / reduce, reuse,
_______________　　환경의 세 가지 R을　　　　　　　　　　　줄이기, 재사용하기,

and recycle.
재활용하기

→ billion은 '10억'이라는 뜻이에요.

2. Every year, / Americans throw away / 27 billion glass bottles, /
매년　　　　　　　미국인들은 버린다　　　　　　270억 개의 유리병을

35 million tons of food, / and 65 million plastic and metal cans.
3500만 톤의 음식을　　　　　　_______________________________

3. Where / does all of this waste / go?
어디로　　이 모든 쓰레기는　　　　　가는 걸까?

4. It all remains / in the land / and takes from 100 to 4,000 years /
그것은 모두 남는다　　땅속에　　　_______________________________

→ decompose는 자연스러운 화학 작용에 의해 '분해되다, 부패되다'라는 뜻이에요.

to decompose.
분해되는 데

→ the best way to...는 '~하는 최선의 방법'이라고 해석해요.

5. The best way / to help the environment / is to reduce the amount of
최선의 방법은　　　　환경에 도움이 되는　　　　_______________________

→ we produce는 앞에 나온 waste를 꾸며줘요. waste 뒤에 관계대명사 which가 생략된 구조예요.

waste / we produce.
_______　우리가 만들어 내는

→ that은 관계대명사로서 that절이 products를 꾸며주고 있어요.

6. We should buy / products / that don't have a lot of packaging.
우리는 사야 한다　　　제품들을　　_______________________________

7. Another way / to help the environment / is to reuse things /
또 다른 방법은　　　환경에 도움이 되는　　　　　물건들을 재사용하는 것이다

instead of throwing them away.
____

40

8. Lastly, / recycle things / to create new products / out of the materials /
마지막으로   물건들을 재활용해라   재료들로

from the old ones.
기존 상품들의

> old는 새로운 것으로 대체되기 전의 '예전의, 기존의'라는 뜻이고,
> ones는 앞에 나온 products 대신 쓰인 거예요.

9. We should also look for / products / that contain recycled materials.
우리는 또한 찾아야 한다   제품들을

> that은 관계대명사로서 that절이 앞에 나온
> products를 꾸며주고 있어요.

Grammar Point · take 시간 to 동사원형

본문 쏙 It all remains in the land and **takes** from 100 to 4,000 years **to decompose**.

그것은 모두 땅속에 남아 있다가 분해되는 데 100~4,000년이 걸린다.

take 다음에 시간이 오면 take는 '시간이 걸리다'라는 뜻이에요. 그래서 〈take 시간 to 동사원형〉의 경우에는 '~하는 데 (시간이) ~ 걸리다'라는 의미가 돼요. 따라서 밑줄 친 부분은 '분해되는 데 100~4,000년이 걸린다'라고 해석하면 됩니다.

확인문제 **1** It takes two hours to drive there.

2 It takes thirty minutes to clean this room.

Alice's Adventures in Wonderland

Alice saw white roses growing in a garden. Three playing cards were busily painting some white roses red. Alice was curious about this.

"Why are you painting the white roses red?" asked Alice.

"The Queen of Hearts wants all roses to be red," the Five of Spades answered.

Then the Queen of Hearts and the playing card soldiers came to the garden. The Queen checked the roses and said to the playing card soldiers, "Off with their heads!"

Alice was angry. "No, you can't do that!" said Alice.

"Yes, I can! Off with your head, too," said the Queen.

"No, no, no!" said Alice.

Suddenly, Alice's sister woke Alice up. Alice realized it was just a strange dream. It was Alice's adventures in Wonderland!

- **garden** 정원
- **playing card** (놀이용) 카드, 트럼프
- **busily** 바쁘게
- **paint** 칠하다
- **queen** 여왕
- **heart** (카드의) 하트
- **spade** (카드의) 스페이드
- **check** 확인하다
- **off with** ~을 떼어라, 베어라
- **woke up** 깨웠다 (wake up 깨우다)
- **realize** 깨닫다
- **adventure** 모험
- **wonderland** 이상한 나라

Comprehension Check

A 문장을 읽고 옳으면 T(True), 틀리면 F(False)에 동그라미 하세요.

1 Three playing cards were busily painting some red roses white.   **T / F**

2 The Queen of Hearts wanted all roses to be red.   **T / F**

3 Alice lived in Wonderland with her sister.   **T / F**

B 다음을 읽고 알맞은 답을 고르세요.

1 This passage is mainly about ________________.

  ⓐ the playing card soldiers

  ⓑ Alice's adventures in Wonderland

  ⓒ The Queen of Hearts

2 Why did Alice get angry at the Queen of Hearts?

  ⓐ Because the playing cards didn't finish painting the roses.

  ⓑ Because the Queen ordered her soldiers to cut off the worker's heads.

  ⓒ Because the Queen woke Alice up.

3 What happened after Alice met the Queen of Hearts?

  ⓐ Three playing cards were dead.

  ⓑ Alice and three playing cards were jailed in a prison.

  ⓒ Alice woke up and realized it was a dream.

C 문장을 완성하는 단어를 써 넣으세요.

1 The Queen of Hearts and the playing card __________ came to the garden.

2 The Queen __________ the roses and said to the playing card soldiers,

"__________ with their heads!"

3 Suddenly, Alice's sister __________ Alice up.

● 잘 읽고 이해했나요? 문장의 정확한 의미를 알아보세요.

1. Alice saw white roses / growing in a garden.
앨리스는 흰 장미들을 보았다　　　　　　______________________

→ playing card는 52장으로 된 '놀이용 카드'로 '트럼프 카드'라고도 해요.

2. Three playing cards / were busily painting / some white roses / red.
세 장의 트럼프 카드들이　　______________________　흰 장미들을　　빨갛게

3. Alice was curious / about this.
______________________　이것에 대해

4. "Why are you painting / the white roses red?" / asked Alice.
______________________　흰 장미들을 빨갛게　　앨리스가 물었다

→ 〈want A to B〉는 'A가 B하기를 원하다'라는 뜻이에요.

5. "The Queen of Hearts / wants all roses to be red," / the Five of Spades
하트의 여왕은　　______________________　스페이드 5가 대답했다

answered.

6. Then the Queen of Hearts / and the playing card soldiers /
그때 하트의 여왕이　　　　　그리고 카드 병정들이

came to the garden.
____

7. The Queen checked the roses / and said to the playing card soldiers, /
______________________　그리고 카드 병정들에게 말했다

"Off with their heads!"
저들의 목을 베어라

8. Alice was angry.　"No, you can't do that!" / said Alice.
앨리스는 화가 났다　　안 돼요, 당신은 그럴 수 없어요　　앨리스가 말했다

→ 이런 상황에서 우리말로는 '아니'라고 하지만, 영어에서는 I can이 긍정문이므로 Yes를 사용해요.

9. "Yes, I can! / Off with your head, too," / said the Queen.
아니, 나는 할 수 있어　______________________　여왕이 말했다

10. "No, no, no!" / said Alice.

안 돼, 안 돼, 안 돼　　　앨리스가 말했다

11. Suddenly, / Alice's sister / woke Alice up.

갑자기　　　　앨리스의 언니가　　　________________

12. Alice realized / it was just a strange dream.

앨리스는 깨달았다　　　________________________________

13. It was Alice's adventures / in Wonderland!

________________________________　　　이상한 나라에서의

Grammar Point　**want A to B**

본문 쏙 The Queen of Hearts **wants** all roses **to** be red.

하트의 여왕은 모든 장미들이 빨간색이기를 원한다.

〈want A(목적어) to B(동사원형)〉는 'A가 B하기를 원하다'라는 뜻이에요. 그래서 want all roses to be red는 '모든 장미들이 빨갛게 되기를 원한다'라고 해석해요. 여왕이 빨갛게 되는 것을 원하는 게 아니라 모든 장미들이 빨갛게 되는 것을 원한다는 의미입니다.

확인문제 **1** I want the room to be clean.

2 Jane didn't want her vacation to end.

A Pioneer in Tech Industry

Bill Gates is an American computer programmer who is the co-founder of Microsoft, one of the largest PC software companies in the world. His work with computers has made a big difference around the world.

Bill was born as the son of a successful lawyer in 1955. Young Bill was a bright and curious boy. He wrote his first computer program as a young teenager. Bill entered Harvard University to study law, but he spent most of his time on computers. In 1975, he dropped out of Harvard to start a software company with his friend Paul Allen. That company was Microsoft.

Bill Gates wasn't afraid to take risks. He had confidence in himself and his products.

- **programmer** 프로그래머
- **co-founder** 공동 창립자
- **software** 소프트웨어
- **company** 회사
- **successful** 성공한
- **lawyer** 변호사
- **bright** 똑똑한
- **wrote** 썼다 (write 쓰다)
- **teenager** 십대
- **enter** 입학하다
- **spent** (시간을) 보냈다 (spend (시간을) 보내다)
- **drop out of** 자퇴하다
- **take a risk** 위험을 감수하다, 모험을 하다
- **confidence** 자신감

Comprehension Check

A 문장을 읽고 옳으면 T(True), 틀리면 F(False)에 동그라미 하세요.

1 Bill Gates is an American computer programmer.　　　**T / F**

2 Bill was a successful lawyer.　　　**T / F**

3 Bill started a software company with his friend.　　　**T / F**

B 다음을 읽고 알맞은 답을 고르세요.

1 This passage is mainly about _______________.

    ⓐ Microsoft

    ⓑ computer programs

    ⓒ Bill Gates

2 What title does NOT describe Bill Gates?

    ⓐ A famous lawyer

    ⓑ A co-founder of Microsoft

    ⓒ A computer programmer

3 Why did Bill Gates drop out of Harvard University?

    ⓐ To write his first computer program

    ⓑ To make money and be a wealthy person

    ⓒ To start a software company, Microsoft, with his friend

C 문장을 완성하는 단어를 써 넣으세요.

1 He wrote his first computer program as a young ___________.

2 Bill ___________ Harvard University to study law, but he spent most of his time on ___________.

3 Bill Gates wasn't afraid to take ___________.

Read and Understand

● 잘 읽고 이해했나요? 문장의 정확한 의미를 알아보세요.

1. Bill Gates is / an American computer programmer / who is the
빌 게이츠는 ~이다

one of the ~ companies는 앞에 나온 Microsoft에 대한 설명이에요.

co-founder of Microsoft, / one of the largest PC software companies in
마이크로소프트의 공동창립자인　　　세계에서 가장 큰 PC 소프트웨어 회사들 중 하나인

the world.

make a difference는 '변화를 일으키다'라는 관용 표현이에요.

2. His work with computers / has made a big difference / around the world.
그가 컴퓨터로 한 일은　　　　큰 변화를 가져왔다

3. Bill was born / as the son / of a successful lawyer / in 1955.
빌은 태어났다　　　아들로　　　　　　　　　　　　　1955년에

4. Young Bill was / a bright and curious boy.
어린 빌은 ~였다

여기서 as는 '~일 때'라는 뜻이고, teenager는
13~19세의 '십대 청소년'을 가리켜요.

5. He wrote / his first computer program / as a young teenager.
그는 썼다　　　　　　　　　　　　　어린 십대 시절에

spend (시간) on...은 '~에 (시간)을 보내다'라는 뜻이에요.

6. Bill entered / Harvard University / to study law, / but he spent most of
빌은 입학했다　　하버드 대학교에　　　법을 공부하기 위해

his time / on computers.
　　　　컴퓨터를 하며

7. In 1975, / he dropped out of Harvard / to start a software company /
1975년에　　　　　　　　　　　　　　소프트웨어 회사를 창업하기 위해

with his friend Paul Allen.
그의 친구 폴 앨런과 함께

8. That company / was Microsoft.
그 회사가　　　마이크로소프트였다

9. Bill Gates wasn't afraid / to take risks.

빌 게이츠는 두려워하지 않았다

10. He had confidence / in himself and his products.

그 자신과 그의 제품들에

Grammar Point 명사(사람)를 뒤에서 꾸며주는 **who**절

본문 쏙 Bill Gates is an American computer <u>programmer **who** is the co-founder of Microsoft</u>.

빌 게이츠는 마이크로소프트의 공동 창립자인 미국의 컴퓨터 프로그래머이다.

who는 programmer를 설명하기 위해 쓰인 관계대명사예요. 즉, who절이 programmer를 꾸며주고 있어요. 따라서 밑줄 친 부분은 '마이크로소프트의 공동 창립자인 프로그래머'라고 해석하면 돼요. 꾸밈 받는 명사가 사물일 때는 관계대명사 which를 사용하지만, programmer처럼 사람일 때는 관계대명사 who를 사용해요. 참고로 관계대명사 that은 사람·사물 관계 없이 모두 쓸 수 있어요.

확인문제

1 The boy who is playing basketball is cute.

2 John is an Australian actor who is the owner of this store.

Visiting New York

My brother Kevin and I visited Aunt Ann, who lives in New York City. This was our first visit to New York, so we wanted to see many landmarks.

On the first day, we took a bus and went to Central Park. It is a public park which is located in Manhattan. It is huge, and we saw lakes, fountains, and bridges.

On the second day, we took a ferry to visit the Statue of Liberty. It is a huge statue on Liberty Island in New York Harbor. We went to the top of the statue in an elevator.

On the third day, we took a taxi and went to New York Times Square. We saw many people and buildings. We watched a famous musical. We had lots of fun with Aunt Ann.

- **aunt** 이모, 고모
- **public** 공공의
- **huge** 거대한
- **fountain** 분수
- **second** 두 번째의
- **ferry** 여객선
- **statue** 조각상
- **liberty** 자유
- **island** 섬
- **harbor** 항구
- **elevator** 엘리베이터
- **third** 세 번째의
- **square** 광장
- **building** 건물
- **watch** 보다, 구경하다
- **musical** 뮤지컬

Comprehension Check

A 문장을 읽고 옳으면 T(True), 틀리면 F(False)에 동그라미 하세요.

1   It was Aunt Ann's first visit to New York City.   **T / F**

2   Central Park is located in Manhattan.   **T / F**

3   Kevin and I took a bus to the top of the Statue of Liberty.   **T / F**

B 다음을 읽고 알맞은 답을 고르세요.

1   This passage is mainly about ________________.

   ⓐ visiting an aunt's house

   ⓑ visiting the island

   ⓒ visiting New York City

2   Where did they go on the first day?

   ⓐ The Statue of Liberty

   ⓑ New York Times Square

   ⓒ Central Park

3   Which type of transportation did Kevin and I NOT take?

   ⓐ A subway   ⓑ A ferry   ⓒ A taxi

C 문장을 완성하는 단어를 써 넣으세요.

1   Central Park is a public park which is __________ in Manhattan.

2   The Statue of Liberty is a huge statue on Liberty Island in New York

   __________.

3   On the __________ day, we __________ a taxi and went to New York

   Times Square.

Read and Understand

● 잘 읽고 이해했나요? 문장의 정확한 의미를 알아보세요.

who는 Aunt Ann에 대해 설명하는 관계대명사예요.

1. My brother Kevin and I / visited Aunt Ann, / who lives in New York
   우리 형 케빈과 나는 　　　　　　　　　앤 이모를 방문했다

   City.

   visit은 '방문하다'라는 동사로도 쓰이고 '방문'이라는 명사로도 쓰여요.

2. This was our first visit / to New York, / so we wanted / to see /
   　　　　　　　　　　　　뉴욕으로　　　　　그래서 우리는 원했다　　보는 것을

   many landmarks.
   많은 랜드마크들을

   교통수단을 '타다'라고 할 때는 동사 take를 주로 사용해요.

3. On the first day, / we took a bus / and went to Central Park.
   첫째 날에　　　　　　　　　　　　　　그리고 센트럴 파크로 갔다

   which는 park를 꾸며주는 관계대명사이고, be located in은 '~에 위치하다'라는 뜻이에요.

4. It is a public park / which is located in Manhattan.
   그것은 공공 공원이다

5. It is huge, / and we saw / lakes, fountains, and bridges.
   그것은 거대하다　　그리고 우리는 봤다

6. On the second day, / we took a ferry / to visit the Statue of Liberty.
   둘째 날에　　　　　　　　우리는 여객선을 탔다

   섬 앞에는 전치사 in이 아니라 on을 써요.

7. It is a huge statue / on Liberty Island / in New York Harbor.
   　　　　　　　　　　　리버티 섬에 있는　　　　뉴욕항의

8. We went / to the top of the statue / in an elevator.
   우리는 갔다　　　　　　　　　　　　　엘리베이터를 타고

9. On the third day, / we took a taxi / and went / to New York Times
   　　　　　　　　　　우리는 택시를 탔다　　그리고 갔다　　뉴욕 타임스퀘어로

   Square.

10. We saw / many people and buildings.

우리는 봤다

→ 야구경기나 뮤지컬처럼 오랜 시간 지켜보는 것에는 동사 watch를 사용해요.

11. We watched / a famous musical.

우리는 관람했다

12. We had lots of fun / with Aunt Ann.

앤 이모와 함께

Grammar Point — **see와 watch의 차이**

본문 쏙 We **saw** many people and buildings. We **watched** a famous musical.

우리는 많은 사람들과 건물들을 봤다. 유명한 뮤지컬도 관람했다.

동사 see와 watch는 둘 다 '보다'라는 뜻이지만 쓰이는 상황이 달라요. see는 무언가를 우연히 보거나 눈에 띄어서 보는 것을 말해요. 반면 watch는 의지를 가지고 오랜 시간 동안 주의 깊게 지켜보는 것을 말해요. 그래서 TV나 뮤지컬, 운동 경기 등을 보는 상황에는 주로 watch를 사용해요.

확인문제

1 I opened the window and saw beautiful trees.

2 He is going to watch a soccer game.

Up 3 to부정사 해석하기 – 명사적 용법과 형용사적 용법

무엇은　어떤　　　　　　　　　　　　　~이다　~하는 것

The best way / **to help** the environment / **is** / **to reduce** the amount of waste.
최선의 방법은　　　　　　환경을 돕기 위한　　　　　　쓰레기의 양을 줄이는 것이다

해설 환경을 돕는 가장 좋은 방법은 쓰레기의 양을 줄이는 것이에요.

way 뒤에 to부정사가 함께 쓰이면 '~을 하기 위한 방법'이라고 해석해요. 앞의 to부정사 to help는 '~하기 위한'이라는 형용사 역할로 해석하고, is 뒤의 to부정사 to reduce는 '~하는 것'이라고 명사 역할로 해석해요.

A 문장을 슬래시(/)로 끊어 읽은 후 우리말 해석을 완성하세요.

1 The best way to enjoy a sunny day is to have a picnic.

→ 최선의 방법은 / ＿＿＿＿＿＿＿＿＿＿＿＿ / 소풍을 가는 것이다

2 A good way to learn new things is to ask questions.

→ 좋은 방법은 / ＿＿＿＿＿＿＿＿＿＿＿ / 질문을 하는 것이다

3 The only way to make friends is to start a conversation.

→ 유일한 방법은 / ＿＿＿＿＿＿＿＿＿＿＿ / 대화를 시작하는 것이다

B 다음 우리말 문장과 일치하도록 영어문장을 알맞게 배열하세요.

1 스트레스를 줄이는 좋은 방법은 음악을 듣는 것이다.

(is / a good way / to reduce stress / to listen to music)

→ ＿＿＿＿＿＿＿＿＿＿＿＿＿＿＿＿＿＿＿＿＿＿＿＿＿.

2 감정을 표현하는 재미있는 방법은 그림을 그리는 것이다.

(to draw pictures / to express feelings / a fun way / is)

→ ＿＿＿＿＿＿＿＿＿＿＿＿＿＿＿＿＿＿＿＿＿＿＿＿＿.

Up 4 지각동사 뒤에 현재분사가 오는 문장 해석하기

누가 / 한다 / 무엇을 / ~하는

Alice / saw / white roses / growing in a garden.
앨리스는　　보았다　　흰 장미들을　　　정원에서 자라고 있는

해설 앨리스는 정원에서 자라고 있는 흰 장미들을 봤어요.

'주어+동사+목적어+목적보어' 구조로 이루어진 5형식 문장이에요. 동사 see는 목적어 다음에 목적어의 동작이나 상태를 설명하는 현재분사(-ing)와 자주 쓰여요. 현재분사 growing이 목적어 white roses의 상태를 설명하여, 정원에서 '자라고 있는' 흰 장미들을 보았다고 해석해요.

A 문장을 슬래시(/)로 끊어 읽은 후 우리말 해석을 완성하세요.

1 Janet saw flowers blooming in the garden.

→ 자넷은 / 보았다 / 꽃들을 / ___________________________

2 They saw birds flying in the sky.

→ 그들은 / 보았다 / 새들을 / ___________________________

3 I saw a child playing in the park.

→ 나는 / 보았다 / 한 아이를 / ___________________________

B 다음 우리말 문장과 일치하도록 영어문장을 알맞게 배열하세요.

1 우리는 나뭇잎들이 나무에서 떨어지는 것을 보았다.

(from the trees / saw / falling / we / the leaves)

→ ____.

2 그들은 비가 온 후 무지개가 나타나는 것을 보았다.

(a rainbow / they / appearing / saw / after the rain)

→ ____.

Icy Land: Antarctica

Antarctica is the southernmost continent on the earth, and the South Pole is found there. Most of Antarctica is covered in ice, and it has almost 90% of all the world's ice.

Antarctica is the coldest continent on the earth. The average summer temperature is −27.5°C, and the average winter temperature is −60°C. People don't permanently reside in Antarctica because of the harsh living conditions. Most people who live there are scientists. They study the weather, animals, glaciers, and the earth's atmosphere.

There are well-known animals that live in Antarctica. Whales, penguins, and seals live there. They mostly depend on krill, so krill are an important source of food in Antarctica.

- **Antarctica** 남극 대륙
- **southernmost** 최남단의
- **continent** 대륙
- **South Pole** 남극
- **average** 평균의
- **permanently** 영구적으로
- **reside** 거주하다
- **harsh** 혹독한
- **conditions** (생활) 환경
- **scientist** 과학자
- **atmosphere** (지구의) 대기
- **well-known** 잘 알려진
- **mostly** 주로
- **depend on** ~에 의존하다
- **krill** 크릴새우
- **source** 원천, 근원

A 문장을 읽고 옳으면 T(True), 틀리면 F(False)에 동그라미 하세요.

1 The South Pole is in Antarctica.   **T / F**

2 Almost 90% of the world's ice is in Antarctica.   **T / F**

3 The living conditions are very nice in Antarctica.   **T / F**

B 다음을 읽고 알맞은 답을 고르세요.

1 This passage is mainly about ________________.

ⓐ the South Pole   ⓑ Antarctica   ⓒ krill

2 What kind of people mostly live in Antarctica?

ⓐ Scientists   ⓑ Fishermen   ⓒ Photographers

3 What is true about Antarctica?

ⓐ It is the hottest continent on the earth.

ⓑ The North Pole can be found there.

ⓒ It is the southernmost continent on the earth.

C 문장을 완성하는 단어를 써 넣으세요.

1 People don't permanently __________ in Antarctica because of the harsh living conditions.

2 Antarctica is the __________ continent on the earth.

3 The average winter __________ is −60℃.

Read and Understand

● 잘 읽고 이해했나요? 문장의 정확한 의미를 알아보세요.

→ Antarctica, South Pole 등의 지명은 항상 첫 글자를 대문자로 표기해요.

1. Antarctica is / the southernmost continent / on the earth, /
남극 대륙은 ~이다 　　　　　　　　　　　　　　　　지구에서

→ is found는 수동태이므로 '발견된다'라고 해석해요.

and the South Pole / is found there.
그리고 남극은 　　　　　　거기서 발견된다

→ be covered in은 '~로 덮여 있다'라는 뜻의 수동태 구문이에요.

2. Most of Antarctica / is covered in ice, / and it has almost 90% /
남극 대륙의 대부분은 　　　　　　　　　　그리고 그것은 거의 90%를 가지고 있다

of all the world's ice.
전 세계 얼음의

3. Antarctica is / the coldest continent / on the earth.
남극 대륙은 ~이다 　　　　　　　　　　　지구에서

4. The average summer temperature / is –27.5°C, / and the average
여름의 평균 기온은 　　　　　　　　　영하 27.5도이다

winter temperature / is –60°C.
　　　　　　　　　영하 60도이다

5. People don't permanently reside / in Antarctica / because of the harsh
사람들은 영구적으로 거주하지 않는다 　　　남극 대륙에서

living conditions.

→ who는 people을 꾸며주는 관계대명사이고, 이 문장의 주어는 Most부터 there까지예요.

6. Most people who live there / are scientists.
　　　　　　　　　　　　　과학자들이다

7. They study / the weather, animals, glaciers, / and the earth's atmosphere.
그들은 연구한다 　날씨, 동물들, 빙하들,

→ that은 animals를 꾸며주는 관계대명사예요.

8. There are / well-known animals / that live in Antarctica.
있다 　　　　　　　　　　　　남극 대륙에 사는

9. Whales, penguins, and seals / live there.

_______________________ 그곳에 산다

10. They mostly depend on krill, / so krill are an important source of food /

_______________________ 그래서 크릴새우는 중요한 식량 원천이다

in Antarctica.

남극 대륙에서

 because of

 People don't permanently reside in Antarctica because of the harsh living conditions.

혹독한 생활 환경 때문에 사람들은 남극 대륙에서 영구적으로 거주하지 않는다.

'~때문에'라는 뜻으로 because를 쓸 때도 있고, because of를 쓸 때도 있어요. 뒤에 나오는 이유가 절(주어+동사)일 때는 because를 쓰지만, 이유가 단어나 구일 때는 because of를 사용해요. 여기서는 이유가 the harsh living conditons라는 구 형태이기 때문에 because of를 쓴 거예요.

 1 Many students were absent from school because of the flu.

2 I'm so tired because of the long flight.

William Tell

Baron Gessler was a mean governor who wanted to test the loyalty of the citizens. To do so, he had his hat hung on a pole and everyone passing had to bow to the hat in order to show their respect.

One day, William Tell passed the hat with his young son, Carl. But he didn't bow to the hat. Immediately, he was arrested. As punishment, Gessler told Tell to shoot an apple on his son's head. Tell's son was placed against a tree, and an apple was put on his head.

Tell took two arrows out, and shot one arrow at his son. It went through the apple. Gessler asked Tell why he had another arrow. Tell told Gessler that if the first arrow killed his son, he was going to shoot the second arrow into Gessler's heart.

- **baron** 남작 (귀족의 최하위 계급)
- **mean** 못된
- **governor** (식민지의) 총독
- **loyalty** 충성
- **citizen** 시민, 주민
- **hung** hang(걸다)의 과거분사
- **pole** 막대기, 장대
- **pass** 지나가다
- **had to** ~해야 했다 (have to ~해야 한다)
- **bow** 절하다
- **in order to** ~하기 위해
- **respect** 존경심
- **immediately** 즉시
- **arrest** 체포하다
- **punishment** 벌, 형벌
- **place** 놓다, 두다

Comprehension Check

A 문장을 읽고 옳으면 T(True), 틀리면 F(False)에 동그라미 하세요.

1 Everyone passing had to bow to the governor. **T / F**

2 William Tell was arrested. **T / F**

3 Tell's son was placed against a tree with an apple on his head. **T / F**

B 다음을 읽고 알맞은 답을 고르세요.

1 This passage is mainly about _______________.

ⓐ Baron Gessler

ⓑ William Tell

ⓒ a hat hung on a pole

2 How many arrows did William Tell take out?

ⓐ Two arrows

ⓑ Three arrows

ⓒ Four arrows

3 Why did Baron Gessler have his hat hung on a pole?

ⓐ To test the loyalty of the citizens

ⓑ To choose the best archer in the town

ⓒ To catch William Tell and his son, Carl

C 문장을 완성하는 단어를 써 넣으세요.

1 As ___________, Gessler told Tell to shoot an apple on his son's head.

2 Tell took two arrows out, and ___________ one arrow at his son.

3 Gessler ___________ Tell why he had another arrow.

Read and Understand

● 잘 읽고 이해했나요? 문장의 정확한 의미를 알아보세요.

1. Baron Gessler was a mean governor / who wanted to test /

→ who는 governor를 꾸며주는 관계대명사예요.

게슬러 남작은 못된 총독이었다　　　시험하고 싶어 했던

the loyalty of the citizens.

2. To do so, / he had his hat hung / on a pole / and everyone passing /

→ hung은 hang(걸다)의 과거분사예요.

그렇게 하기 위해서　그는 그의 모자를 걸어 놓게 했다　장대에　그리고 지나가는 모든 사람들은

had to bow to the hat / in order to show / their respect.

보여주기 위해　그들의 존경심을

3. One day, / William Tell passed the hat / with his young son, Carl.

어느 날　윌리엄 텔이 그 모자를 지나갔다

4. But / he didn't bow to the hat.

그러나　그는 그 모자에 절하지 않았다

5. Immediately, / he was arrested.

→ was arrested는 수동태이므로 '체포됐다'라고 해석해요.

즉시

6. As punishment, / Gessler told Tell / to shoot an apple / on his son's head.

벌로써　게슬러는 텔에게 말했다　그의 아들의 머리 위에 있는

7. Tell's son was placed / against a tree, / and an apple was put /

→ was placed와 was put은 수동태이므로 각각 '세워졌다', '놓여졌다'라고 해석해요.

텔의 아들은 세워졌다　나무에 등을 대고

on his head.

그의 머리 위에

8. Tell took two arrows out, / and shot one arrow / at his son.

→ shot은 shoot(쏘다)의 과거형이에요.

그리고 화살 한 개를 쐈다　그의 아들을 향해

9. It went through / the apple.

→ went through는 go through(통과하다, 관통하다)의 과거형이에요.

사과를

10. Gessler asked Tell / why he had another arrow.

게슬러는 텔에게 물었다 _______________________________

11. Tell told Gessler that / if the first arrow killed his son, /

텔이 게슬러에게 ~라고 말했다 _______________________________

he was going to shoot the second arrow / into Gessler's heart.

그는 두 번째 화살을 쏘려고 했다 　　　　　　　게슬러의 심장으로

Grammar Point	**have + A + 과거분사**

본문 쏙 
To do so, he had his hat hung on a pole.

이를 위해 그는 장대에 그의 모자를 걸어 놓게 했다.

〈have+A(목적어)+과거분사〉는 'A가 ~되게 하다'라는 뜻이에요. 그래서 had his hat hung은 '그의 모자가 걸리게 했다'라고 해석하면 돼요. 모자가 스스로 거는 것이 아니라 모자가 누군가에 의해 걸리는 것이므로 수동의 의미를 갖는 과거분사 hung을 쓴 거예요.

확인문제 **1** He had his car fixed.

2 I had my shirts dry-cleaned yesterday.

Color Therapy

How do you feel when you see the color red? Do you feel angry? How about blue? Does it make you feel smart? Different colors make you feel different emotions. When colors are used to make people feel a certain way, this is called "color therapy."

You probably don't like to go to the dentist's office. Who does? Dentists use color therapy to make their patients feel better. They might paint the walls green or yellow. Green makes the patients feel calm and secure. Yellow helps the patients feel bright and cheery.

Some therapists use colors to help people overcome negative emotions. They shine colored lights on patients, or wrap their bodies in colored silks. They try to make the patients feel happier, more energetic, or more relaxed.

- **emotion** 감정
- **certain** 특정한
- **therapy** 치료, 요법
- **dentist** 치과의사
- **patient** 환자
- **calm** 침착한
- **secure** 안심하는
- **cheery** 쾌활한
- **therapist** 치료사
- **overcome** 극복하다
- **negative** 부정적인
- **shine** 빛을 비추다
- **colored** 색깔이 있는
- **wrap** 감싸다
- **silk** 실크, 비단
- **energetic** 활기찬
- **relaxed** 편안한

Comprehension Check

A 문장을 읽고 옳으면 T(True), 틀리면 F(False)에 동그라미 하세요.

1 Different colors make you feel different emotions. **T / F**

2 The patients feel cheery when the walls are blue. **T / F**

3 Some therapists use colors to help people overcome
negative emotions. **T / F**

B 다음을 읽고 알맞은 답을 고르세요.

1 This passage is mainly about ________________.
   ⓐ different emotions
   ⓑ color therapy
   ⓒ dentists

2 According to the story, which color makes people feel calm and secure?
   ⓐ Yellow　　　　ⓑ Blue　　　　ⓒ Green

3 How do the therapists use colors to help patients?
   ⓐ They shine colored lights on patients.
   ⓑ They paint the wall red.
   ⓒ They give patients some yellow medicine.

C 문장을 완성하는 단어를 써 넣으세요.

1 Dentists use color therapy to make their __________ feel better.

2 Dentists might paint the walls __________ or __________.

3 Therapists try to make the patients feel happier, more __________, or
more relaxed.

Read and Understand

● 잘 읽고 이해했나요? 문장의 정확한 의미를 알아보세요.

1. How do you feel / when you see the color red?   Do you feel angry?
_____________________ 빨간색을 보면   화가 나는가?

→ make you feel...은 '너를 ~하게 느끼게 하다'라고 해석해요.

2. How about blue?   Does it make you / feel smart?
파란색은 어떤가?   그것은 당신을 만드는가?   _____________

3. Different colors / make you / feel different emotions.
다른 색깔들은   당신을 만든다   _____________________

a certain way는 '특정한 방식'이라는 뜻이에요.

4. When colors are used / to make people / feel a certain way, /
_____________________ 사람들을 만들기 위해   특정한 방식을 느끼도록

this is called / "color therapy."
이것은 불린다   "색채 요법"이라고

5. You probably don't like / to go to the dentist's office.   Who does?
_____________________ 치과에 가는 것을   누군들 좋아하겠는가?

6. Dentists use / color therapy / to make their patients feel better.
치과 의사들은 사용한다   색채 요법을   _____________________

→ might는 '~할지도 모른다'라는 뜻의 조동사예요.

7. They might paint / the walls / green or yellow.
_____________________ 벽을   초록색이나 노란색으로

8. Green makes / the patients / feel calm and secure.
초록색은 만든다   환자들을   _____________________

cheery는 cheerful(명랑한, 쾌활한)과 같은 뜻이에요.

9. Yellow helps / the patients / feel bright and cheery.
노란색은 도와준다   환자들을   _____________________

10. Some therapists use colors / to help people / overcome negative emotions.
어떤 치료사들은 색깔들을 사용한다   사람들을 도와주기 위해   _____________________

11. They shine / colored lights / on patients, / or wrap their bodies /

그들은 비춘다   색이 있는 빛을   환자들에게

in colored silks.

색이 있는 실크로

3음절 이상의 긴 형용사는 비교급을 만들 때 앞에 more를 붙여요. ←

12. They try / to make the patients feel / happier, more energetic,

그들은 노력한다   환자들이 느끼도록 만들려고

과거분사에서 온 형용사도 비교급을 만들 때 앞에 more를 붙여요.

or more relaxed.

Grammar Point **when의 쓰임**

본문 쏙 How do you feel **when** you see the color red?

빨간색을 보면 당신은 어떻게 느끼는가?

이 문장에서 when은 '~할 때'라기보다는 '~하면'이라고 해석하는 것이 자연스러워요. 그렇다면 같은 뜻을 가진 if와는 어떻게 다를까요? if는 일어날 가능성이 낮거나 불투명한 일에 대해 사용하고, when은 일어날 가능성이 높거나 예정된 일에 대해 사용한다는 차이가 있답니다.

확인문제 **1** Let me know when you are ready.

2 He works out very hard when he is stressed.

Nick, the Superhero

Nick loved to read superhero stories. He always wanted to be like a superhero. Whenever he did something, he did it like a superhero.

When he ran an errand for his mother, he ran as fast as he could. When he did his homework, he timed himself with a stopwatch. When he cleaned up his room, he moved all of the furniture single-handedly. When he rode his bike to school, he raced against the school bus. When he went to the playground, he didn't play with his friends. He went up to the top of the jungle gym and watched over the other kids.

Nick believed that someday he could help others like a superhero. This is why he trained himself all the time.

- **superhero**
  슈퍼히어로[영웅]
- **whenever**
  ~할 때마다
- **errand** 심부름
- **time** 시간을 재다
- **stopwatch**
  스톱워치
- **furniture** 가구
- **single-handedly**
  혼자 힘으로
- **race** 경주하다
- **playground**
  놀이터
- **jungle gym**
  정글짐
- **watch over**
  지켜보다
- **believe** 믿다
- **train** 훈련시키다

Comprehension Check

A 문장을 읽고 옳으면 T(True), 틀리면 F(False)에 동그라미 하세요.

1 Nick always wanted to be like a superhero.　　　　　　**T / F**

2 Nick ran as fast as he could to run an errand for his mother.　　**T / F**

3 When he rode his bike to school, he raced against other bikes.　**T / F**

B 다음을 읽고 알맞은 답을 고르세요.

1 This passage is mainly about ________________.

　ⓐ a boy watching a superhero

　ⓑ a boy who wanted to be a superhero

　ⓒ a strong boy

2 What did Nick use when he did his homework?

　ⓐ A superhero story book　　　ⓑ A bike　　　ⓒ A stopwatch

3 Why did Nick train himself all the time?

　ⓐ To help others like a superhero someday

　ⓑ To impress his mother

　ⓒ To win the race

C 문장을 완성하는 단어를 써 넣으세요.

1 Nick loved to read __________ stories.

2 He went up to the top of the jungle gym and __________ over the other kids.

3 When he cleaned up his room, he __________ all of the furniture __________.

Read and Understand

● 잘 읽고 이해했나요? 문장의 정확한 의미를 알아보세요.

1. Nick loved / to read superhero stories.

닉은 무척 좋아했다 ________________________

→ like는 '~처럼'이라는 뜻으로 쓰였어요.

2. He always wanted / to be like a superhero.

그는 항상 원했다 ________________________

3. Whenever he did something, / he did it / like a superhero.

________________________ 그는 그것을 했다 슈퍼히어로처럼

↳ run an errand는 '심부름을 하다'라는 뜻이에요.

4. When he ran an errand / for his mother, / he ran / as fast as he could.

그는 심부름을 할 때 그의 엄마를 위해 그는 달렸다 ________________________

→ time은 '시간'이라는 명사 외에 '시간을 재다'라는 동사로도 쓰여요.

5. When he did his homework, / he timed himself / with a stopwatch.

그는 숙제를 할 때 ________________________ 스톱워치를 가지고

furniture는 셀 수 없는 명사이므로 항상 단수로 취급하고 -s/es를 붙이지 않아요. ↰

6. When he cleaned up his room, / he moved / all of the furniture /

________________________ 그는 옮겼다 모든 가구들을

single-handedly.

혼자 힘으로

→ race against는 '~를 상대로 경주하다'라는 뜻이에요.

7. When he rode his bike / to school, / he raced against the school bus.

그는 자전거를 타고 갈 때 학교로 ________________________

8. When he went / to the playground, / he didn't play with his friends.

그는 갔을 때 놀이터로 ________________________

9. He went up / to the top of the jungle gym / and watched over the

그는 올라갔다 정글짐의 꼭대기로 ________________________

other kids.

____

10. Nick believed / that someday he could help others / like a superhero.

닉은 믿었다   ______________________________________   슈퍼히어로로처럼

> This is why...는 '이것이 ~한 이유다', 즉 '그래서 ~이다'라는 뜻이에요.

11. This is why / he trained himself / all the time.

그래서   ________________________   항상

Grammar Point   **as + 형용사/부사 + as + 주어 could**

본문 쏙 When he ran an errand for his mother, he ran as fast as he could.

그는 엄마를 위해 심부름을 할 때 최대한 빨리 달렸다.

〈as 형용사 as〉는 '~만큼 ~한'이라는 뜻이고, 〈as 부사 as〉는 '~만큼 ~하게'라는 뜻이에요. 그래서 as fast as he could는 '그가 달릴 수 있는 만큼 빨리'라는 뜻이고, 이는 곧 '최대한 빨리'라고 해석하면 됩니다.

확인문제 **1** When I ate pizza with my brother, I ate as fast as I could.

2 She spoke as slowly as she could.

Stonehenge

Stonehenge, like the pyramids of Egypt, is an ancient mystery of the world. It is a very strange sight. On a green wide-open plain, huge rectangular stones stand upright, almost 9 meters tall. Other stones are placed on top of them. Who put those stones there? And why?

We may never know exactly why. Part of the reason is that different groups built Stonehenge over 700 years! First, people buried their dead around the circle that they dug into the ground. Later, people put wooden poles in a circle to mark the positions of the sun, moon, and stars. Finally, stones were placed in a circle. Stonehenge started as a graveyard. Later it became a place of worship and mystery.

- **pyramid** 피라미드
- **ancient** 고대의
- **mystery** 미스터리
- **sight** 광경, 모습
- **wide-open** 확 트인
- **plain** 평야
- **rectangular** 직사각형의
- **upright** 똑바른, 수직의
- **exactly** 정확히
- **group** 그룹
- **bury** 묻다
- **dead** 죽은 사람들
- **dug** 팠다 (dig 파다)
- **wooden** 나무로 된
- **mark** 표시하다
- **position** 위치
- **graveyard** 묘지
- **worship** 숭배, 예배

A 문장을 읽고 옳으면 T(True), 틀리면 F(False)에 동그라미 하세요.

1 Stonehenge is an ancient mystery of the world. **T / F**

2 Stonehenge is on the top of a mountain. **T / F**

3 Stonehenge started as a graveyard. **T / F**

B 다음을 읽고 알맞은 답을 고르세요.

1 This passage is mainly about _________________.

   ⓐ the pyramids of Egypt   **ⓑ** stones   **ⓒ** Stonehenge

2 What does Stonehenge look like?

   ⓐ Huge round stones are put in a circle and some trees are growing around them.

   ⓑ Huge rectangular stones stand upright and other stones are placed on top of them.

   ⓒ Some wooden poles are placed in a circle.

3 What is NOT true about Stonehenge?

   ⓐ It is an ancient mystery of the world.

   ⓑ Different groups built it over 700 years.

   ⓒ It started as a place of worship and became a graveyard.

C 문장을 완성하는 단어를 써 넣으세요.

1 On a green wide-open ___________, huge rectangular stones stand ___________, almost 9 meters tall.

2 Later, people put wooden ___________ in a circle to ___________ the positions of the sun, moon and stars.

Read and Understand

● 잘 읽고 이해했나요? 문장의 정확한 의미를 알아보세요.

like the pyramids of Egypt는 Stonehenge를 설명하기
위해 삽입된 구문이에요. 그래서 앞뒤에 쉼표가 있어요.

1. Stonehenge, / like the pyramids of Egypt, / is an ancient mystery of
스톤헨지는　　　　　　　이집트의 피라미드처럼

the world.

2. It is / a very strange sight.
이것은 ~이다

stand upright은 '수직으로 서 있다'라는 뜻이에요.

3. On a green wide-open plain, / huge rectangular stones stand upright, /
확 트인 푸른 평야 위에

almost 9 meters tall.
거의 9미터 높이로

4. Other stones are placed / on top of them.
　　　　　　　　　　　　　　　그것들 위에

5. Who put those stones / there?　And why?
　　　　　　　　　　　　그곳에　　　그리고 왜?

6. We may never know / exactly why.
　　　　　　　　　　　　정확히 왜인지

that절이 is 뒤에서 보어 역할을 하고 있어요.

7. Part of the reason is / that different groups built Stonehenge /
그 이유 중 하나는 ~이다

over 700 years!
700년 넘게

dead는 '죽은'이라는 뜻 외에 '죽은 사람들'이라는 뜻도 있어요.

8. First, / people buried / their dead / around the circle /
먼저　　　사람들은 묻었다　　　죽은 사람들을　　　원을 따라

that은 관계대명사로서 that절이 circle을 꾸며주고 있어요.

that they dug into the ground.

9. Later, / people put / wooden poles / in a circle / to mark the positions /
그런 후에   사람들은 세웠다   나무 막대기들을   동그랗게

of the sun, moon, and stars.
태양, 달, 그리고 별들의

10. Finally, / stones were placed / in a circle.
마지막으로   동그랗게

11. Stonehenge started / as a graveyard.
스톤헨지는 시작했다

12. Later it became / a place of worship and mystery.
나중에 그것은 ~이 되었다

알아두면 문장이 쉽게
이해되는 그래머 포인트

Grammar Point | **쉼표(,)의 역할**

본문 쏙 On a green wide-open plain, huge rectangular stones stand upright, almost 9 meters tall.
확 트인 푸른 평야 위에, 높이가 거의 9미터인 거대한 직사각형 돌들이 수직으로 서 있다.

이 문장은 길고 복잡해 보이지만 쉼표(,)를 기준으로 의미가 나뉘어진다는 점을 알면 쉽게 해석할 수 있어요. On a green wide-open plain이라는 장소를 쉼표로 구분한 다음, 문장의 뼈대인 '주어+동사'가 나옵니다(huge rectangular stones stand upright). 여기에 돌에 대한 설명을 추가하기 위에 쉼표로 구분한 뒤에 almost 9 meters tall이 나온 구조입니다.

확인문제 **1** My best friend, who lives in France, is very smart.

2 After he ran all the way home, he quickly opened the door, and shut it fast.

Up 5 최상급 구문 해석하기

무엇은 ~이다 / 가장 ~한 / ~에서

Antarctica is / **the coldest** continent / **on the earth.**
남극 대륙은 ~이다 / 가장 추운 대륙 / 지구에서

해설 남극 대륙은 지구에서 가장 추운 대륙이에요.

이 문장은 '주어+동사+보어'로 이루어진 2형식 문장이에요. cold에 -est가 붙은 최상급 형용사 coldest가 명사 continent를 수식해 '가장 추운 대륙'이라고 해석해요. 이때, 비교의 범위를 알려주는 전치사구가 함께 쓰이는데 이 문장에서는 남극이 '지구에서' 가장 추운 대륙이라고 설명하고 있어요.

A 문장을 슬래시(/)로 끊어 읽은 후 우리말 해석을 완성하세요.

1 Jack is the smartest student in the class.

→ 잭은 ~이다 / _____________________ / 반에서

2 Steve is the fastest runner on the team.

→ 스티브는 ~이다 / _____________________ / 팀에서

3 This is the clearest lake in the city.

→ 이곳은 ~이다 / _____________________ / 그 도시에서

B 다음 우리말 문장과 일치하도록 영어문장을 알맞게 배열하세요.

1 그는 그 대회에서 가장 재능 있는 가수이다.

(in the competition / the most talented singer / He is)

→ ____.

2 이 곳은 세상에서 가장 아름다운 곳이다.

(this is / in the world / the most beautiful place)

→ ____.

Up **6** 이유를 설명하는 This is why 구문 해석하기

This is why / he trained himself / all the time.
이것이 ~를 하는   그가 스스로를 단련시켰다   항상
이유이다

해설 이것이 그가 항상 스스로를 단련시킨 이유예요. (= 그래서 그는 항상 스스로를 단련시켰어요.)

This is why는 '이것이 ~를 하는 이유이다'라는 뜻으로, 앞에 언급된 이것(This) 때문에 why 뒤에 무엇을 하게 됐는지를 나타낸 문장입니다. 이야기 속에서 닉은 수퍼히어로처럼 자신이 다른 사람을 도울 수 있을 거라고 믿으며, '이 점(this)이 그가 자신을 훈련하는 이유'라고 말합니다. 간략히 '그래서 ~한다'라고 해석할 수 있어요.

A 문장을 슬래시(/)로 끊어 읽은 후 우리말 해석을 완성하세요.

1 This is why we want to join the meeting together.

→ 그래서 / ________________________________ / 함께

2 This is why he drove his car carefully.

→ 그래서 / ________________________________

3 This is why my dad saved more money.

→ 그래서 / ________________________________

B 다음 우리말 문장과 일치하도록 영어문장을 알맞게 배열하세요.

1 그래서 그들이 여행 전에 자전거를 수리했다.

(they repaired the bike / before the trip / this is why)

→ ____.

2 그래서 내가 주말마다 이웃을 돕기로 결심했다.

(this is why / every weekend / I decided to help my neighbor)

→ ____.

Robinson Crusoe

Robinson Crusoe was shipwrecked off the coast of South America. He survived a huge storm and was washed up on the shore of an island. He knew that he was the only survivor of the wreck.

Crusoe wanted to live, so he planned how to get food and shelter to protect himself from wild animals. He searched the wrecked ship and collected food and useful items. He found some biscuits, some dried meat, some alcohol, a spyglass, axes, and some guns.

As time passed, Crusoe constructed many useful things like a canoe and houses. He also learned about farming. After spending about fifteen years on the island, he found a man's footprints. There were men living on the island. Who could they be?

- **shipwrecked**
  난파한, 조난 당한
- **coast** 해안
- **survive** 살아남다
- **wash up** 물이
  (육지로) ~을 쓸고 오다
- **shore** 해안
- **survivor** 생존자
- **wreck**
  난파선; 난파하다
- **shelter** 주거지
- **wild** 야생의
- **search** 수색하다
- **wrecked** 난파된
- **collect** 모으다
- **biscuit** 비스킷
- **alcohol** 술
- **spyglass**
  작은 망원경
- **construct**
  건설하다
- **canoe** 카누
- **farming** 농사
- **footprint** 발자국

Comprehension Check

A 문장을 읽고 옳으면 T(True), 틀리면 F(False)에 동그라미 하세요.

1 The ship wrecked because of a storm.　　　　　　**T / F**

2 Crusoe got some dried meat from the wrecked ship.　　**T / F**

3 Crusoe got off the island after fifteen years.　　　　**T / F**

B 다음을 읽고 알맞은 답을 고르세요.

1 This passage is mainly about ________________.

　ⓐ Robinson Crusoe's survival

　ⓑ the strange island

　ⓒ the coast of South America

2 What did Robinson find on the wrecked ship?

　ⓐ Some bread　　　　ⓑ Knives　　　　ⓒ A spyglass

3 What did Robinson do at first after being washed up on the shore?

　ⓐ He constructed some useful things like houses.

　ⓑ He planned how to get food and shelter.

　ⓒ He searched for human footprints.

C 문장을 완성하는 단어를 써 넣으세요.

1 Crusoe knew that he was the only __________ of the wreck.

2 After spending about __________ years on the island, he found a man's __________.

3 There were men __________ on the island.

Read and Understand

● 잘 읽고 이해했나요? 문장의 정확한 의미를 알아보세요.

1. Robinson Crusoe was shipwrecked / off the coast of South America.
남아메리카 해안에서

2. He survived / a huge storm / and was washed up / on the shore of an
그는 살아남았다   그리고 쓸려 왔다   섬의 해안으로

island.

3. He knew / that he was the only survivor / of the wreck.
그는 알았다   난파선의

〈how to 동사원형〉은 '어떻게 ~하는지', '~하는 방법'이라는 뜻이에요.

4. Crusoe wanted to live, / so he planned / how to get food and shelter /
크루소는 살고 싶었다   그래서 그는 계획했다   어떻게 음식과 대피처를 마련할지

to ~ animals가 shelter를 꾸며주고 있어요.

to protect himself from wild animals.

5. He searched / the wrecked ship / and collected / food and useful items.
그는 뒤졌다   난파선을   그리고 모았다

6. He found / some biscuits, / some dried meat, / some alcohol, /
그는 찾았다   약간의 비스킷   약간의 술

여러 개를 나열할 때 and는 맨 마지막 단어 앞에 넣어요.

a spyglass, / axes, / and some guns.
작은 망원경   도끼들   그리고 총 몇 개를

여기서 as는 접속사로서 '~하는 동안'이라는 의미예요.

7. As time passed, / Crusoe constructed / many useful things /
시간이 흐르는 동안   크루소는 지었다

like a canoe and houses.
카누와 집들 같은

8. He also learned / about farming.
그는 또한 알게 됐다

9. After spending about fifteen years / on the island, / he found /

15년 정도 보낸 후에   섬에서   그는 발견했다

여기서 man은 '남자'가 아닌 '사람'을 뜻해요.

a man's footprints.

men은 man(남자, 사람)의 복수형이에요.

10. There were men / living on the island.

사람들이 있었다

11. Who could they be?

그들은 누구일까?

Grammar Point   find와 look for의 차이

본문 쏙 He **found** some biscuits, some dried meat, some alcohol, a spyglass, axes, and some guns.

그는 약간의 비스킷, 약간의 말린 고기, 술, 작은 망원경, 도끼들, 그리고 총 몇 개를 찾았다.

동사 find와 look for는 둘 다 '찾다'라는 뜻이지만, 사용하는 상황이 달라요. find는 무언가를 '결국 찾아내다'라는 결과에 초점을 둔 단어라면, look for는 무언가를 '찾고 있다, 찾아 보다'라는 행동에 초점을 둔 단어예요. 따라서 look for는 '찾고 있는 중이다'라는 현재 진행형으로 자주 사용된답니다.

확인문제   **1** I found my keys on the table.

2 I am looking for my keys for two hours.

Understanding AI

AI, or Artificial Intelligence, is like a smart computer that can learn and think. It's used in many things we see every day.

For example, when you talk to Siri or Alexa, that's AI helping you. AI can play games, answer questions, and even help doctors find out what's wrong with patients. It can also translate languages, so you can talk to someone who speaks a different language. Think of it as a robot brain that helps people do things faster and better. In schools, AI can help you learn by giving you fun quizzes and games.

While it might sound like science fiction, AI is here to help us in real life, making our lives easier and more fun.

- **artificial** 인공의
- **intelligence** 지능
- **even** 심지어
- **patient** 환자
- **translate** 번역하다
- **language** 언어
- **brain** 뇌
- **sound like** ～처럼 들리다
- **science fiction** 공상 과학 소설
- **real life** 현실, 실제 생활

Comprehension Check

 문장을 읽고 옳으면 T(True), 틀리면 F(False)에 동그라미 하세요.

1 AI is like a smart computer.   **T / F**

2 AI cannot translate the Chinese language into English.   **T / F**

3 AI is difficult to find in our real life.   **T / F**

 다음을 읽고 알맞은 답을 고르세요.

1 This passage is mainly about ________________.

   ⓐ who created AI

   ⓑ how AI can be harmful to people

   ⓒ how AI helps people in everyday life

2 Which is NOT mentioned as an example of how AI is used in the passage?

   ⓐ Helping doctors diagnose patients

   ⓑ Driving cars   ⓒ Translating languages

3 According to the passage, how does AI help in schools?

   ⓐ By teaching students in the classroom

   ⓑ By providing fun quizzes and games for learning

   ⓒ By grading all the students' homework

 문장을 완성하는 단어를 써 넣으세요.

1 When you talk to Siri or Alexa, that's AI __________ you.

2 Think of it as a robot __________ that helps people do things __________ and better.

3 AI is here to help us in __________ life, making our lives easier and more __________.

● 잘 읽고 이해했나요? 문장의 정확한 의미를 알아보세요.

that can learn and think는 관계대명사절로,
앞의 a smart computer를 수식해요. ←

1. AI, or Artificial Intelligence, / is like a smart computer / that can
AI, 또는 인공지능은   똑똑한 컴퓨터와 같다   __________

learn and think.
____

2. It's used / in many things / we see every day.
__________ 많은 것들에   우리가 매일 보는

helping you는 현재분사구로, AI의 기능을 설명해요. ←

3. For example, / when you talk to Siri or Alexa, / that's AI helping you.
__________   당신이 시리나 알렉사에게 말할 때,   __________________

4. AI can play games, / answer questions, / and even help doctors /
AI는 게임을 할 수 있다   __________   그리고 심지어 의사들을 도울 수 있다

→ find out: (몰랐던 것을) 알아내다, 찾아내다

find out / what's wrong with patients.
알아내도록   __________________

so(그래서)는 결과를 나타내는 접속사예요.

5. It can also translate languages, / so you can talk /
__________________________   그래서 당신은 이야기할 수 있다

to someone who speaks a different language.
다른 언어로 말하는 누군가와

→ that helps people do things는 앞의 a robot brain을 수식해요.

6. Think of it / as a robot brain / that helps people / do things /
그것을 생각해봐라   로봇의 뇌로   사람들을 도와주는   __________

faster and better.
____

→ by -ing: ~함으로써

7. In schools, / AI can help / you learn / by giving you /
학교에서   __________   __________   당신에게 제공함으로써

fun quizzes and games.
재미있는 퀴즈와 게임을

8. While it might sound / like science fiction, / AI is here / to help us /

그것이 들릴 수 있지만　　　　　공상 과학 소설처럼　　　　　AI는 여기 있다

in real life, / making our lives / easier and more fun.

현실에서　　　　우리의 삶을 만들면서

Grammar Point　전치사 **by**

본문 쏙 AI can help you learn **by** giving you fun quizzes and games.

AI는 재미있는 퀴즈와 게임을 제공함으로써 당신이 배우는 것을 도울 수 있다.

'by+동사ing' 형태로 오는 경우, '~함으로써' 또는 '~해서'라는 뜻으로 수단 또는 방법을 나타내는 전치사로 해석합니다. 따라서 by giving은 '제공함으로써'라고 해석해요. 뒤에 오는 giving you fun quizzes and games는 그 수단을 구체적으로 설명하는 동명사구예요.

확인문제 **1** Nelly stays healthy by exercising every day.

2 Kevin learned to cook by watching online videos.

Cooking for Myself

I'm Ryan. I'm a junior high school student. My parents run a drugstore, so they need to work until late at night. Since I'm an only child, I often eat dinner alone. My parents let me order pizza or pick up a hamburger from a fast-food place. But now I have gotten tired of eating fast food for dinner all the time.

I learned at school that cooking food for yourself is important. It can prevent obesity and keep you healthy. It can also make you creative and independent. Therefore, I've decided to cook food for myself. Of course I promised my parents that I would be careful with the stove and knives.

I searched the Internet and found some simple recipes. For starters, I'm going to cook an omelet. Why don't you try cooking for yourself?

- **junior high school** 중학교
- **drugstore** 약국
- **alone** 혼자
- **order** 주문하다
- **get tired of** ~에 싫증나다
- **prevent** 예방하다
- **obesity** 비만
- **healthy** 건강한
- **creative** 창의적인
- **independent** 독립적인
- **therefore** 그러므로, 그래서
- **decide** 결심하다
- **promise** 약속하다
- **careful** 조심하는
- **stove** 가스레인지
- **knives** 칼들 (knife 칼)
- **search** 검색하다
- **recipe** 요리법
- **omelet** 오믈렛

86

Comprehension Check

 문장을 읽고 옳으면 T(True), 틀리면 F(False)에 동그라미 하세요.

1 Ryan goes to a junior high school.　　　　　　　**T / F**

2 Ryan doesn't have any brothers or sisters.　　　**T / F**

3 Ryan learned how to cook from his mother.　　　**T / F**

B 다음을 읽고 알맞은 답을 고르세요.

1 This passage is mainly about _______________.

   ⓐ cooking for my parents

   ⓑ cooking for myself

   ⓒ cooking fast food

2 What is Ryan going to cook for dinner?

   ⓐ An omelet　　　　　　**ⓑ** Fried rice　　　　　　**ⓒ** A Hamburger

3 What is a good thing about cooking food for yourself?

   ⓐ We can feel calm and secure.

   ⓑ We can be creative and independent.

   ⓒ We can pass the exam.

C 문장을 완성하는 단어를 써 넣으세요.

1 My parents _________ a drugstore, so they need to work until late at night.

2 I have gotten _________ _________ eating fast food for dinner all the time.

3 I _________ the Internet and found some simple _________.

● 잘 읽고 이해했나요? 문장의 정확한 의미를 알아보세요.

1. I'm Ryan.   I'm a junior high school student.
나는 라이언이다

> run은 약국, 식당, 회사 등을 '운영하다'라는 뜻이 있어요.

2. My parents run a drugstore, / so they need to work / until late at night.
그래서 그들은 일해야 한다　　　밤 늦게까지

> only child는 '외동아이'라는 뜻이에요.

3. Since I'm an only child, / I often eat / dinner alone.
나는 종종 먹는다　　　저녁을 혼자

pick up은 가게에서 물건을 '찾아오다', '사 오다'라는 뜻으로 자주 쓰여요.

4. My parents / let me order pizza / or pick up a hamburger /
우리 부모님은　　　또는 햄버거를 사다 먹으라고

from a fast-food place.
패스트푸드점에서

> get tired of(~에 질리다) 뒤에는 명사나 동명사가 와요. gotten은 get의 과거분사예요.

5. But now / I have gotten tired of / eating fast food / for dinner /
하지만 지금　　　패스트푸드를 먹는 것에　　　저녁으로

all the time.
항상

6. I learned / at school / that / cooking food for yourself / is important.
나는 배웠다　　학교에서　　~라는 것을　　　중요하다

> keep...healthy는 '~를 건강하게 유지해 주다'라는 뜻이에요.

7. It can prevent obesity / and keep you healthy.
그리고 여러분을 건강하게 유지해 준다

8. It can also make you / creative and independent.
그것은 또한 너를 만들어 줄 수 있다

9. Therefore, / I've decided / to cook food for myself.
그래서　　　나는 결심했다

10. Of course / I promised my parents / that I would be careful /

물론 조심하겠다고

with the stove and knives.

가스레인지와 칼을 다룰 때

11. I searched the Internet / and found / some simple recipes.

그리고 발견했다　　몇 가지 간단한 요리법을

for starters는 '우선 먼저'라는 뜻이에요.

12. For starters, / I'm going to cook / an omelet.

우선 가장 먼저 오믈렛을

try -ing는 '~을 시도해 보다, 도전해 보다'라는 뜻이에요.

13. Why don't you / try cooking / for yourself?

~하는 게 어때?　　요리해 보는 게

알아두면 문장이 쉽게
이해되는 그래머 포인트

Grammar Point　**let A B**

본문 쏙 My parents let me order pizza or pick up a hamburger from a fast-food place.

우리 부모님은 내게 피자를 주문하거나 패스트푸드점에서 햄버거를 사다 먹으라고 하셨다.

let은 '~하게 하다, ~하게 시키다'라는 뜻이에요. 그래서 〈let A(목적어) B(동사원형)〉 형태는 'A가 B 하게 하다/시키다'라고 해석해요. 예문의 let me order는 '내가 주문하게 하다', let me pick up은 '내가 사다 먹게 하다'라는 뜻이에요.

확인문제 **1** My teacher let us listen to music in class.

2 She let them eat ice cream for dessert.

frog eggs

tadpole

tadpole with legs

frog

froglet

Frogs

Have you ever seen frog eggs floating in a pond? Frogs lay up to 4,000 eggs at one time. But most of them won't hatch. Some of the eggs will be eaten by other animals, and other eggs might dry up in the sun or break in the water.

The eggs hatch after about seven days and the life cycle of tadpoles begins. A tadpole begins to swim and eat algae. Six weeks after the hatch, a tadpole grows hind legs and a longer tail. It eats tiny insects.

Nine weeks after the hatch, a tadpole looks like a baby frog but with a tail. It's called a froglet or a young frog. At week sixteen, a froglet loses its tail and becomes an adult frog.

- **float** (물에) 떠 있다
- **pond** 연못
- **lay** (알을) 낳다
- **hatch** 부화하다; 부화
- **eaten** eat(먹다)의 과거분사
- **dry up** 바싹 마르다
- **break** 부서지다
- **tadpole** 올챙이
- **life cycle** 생애주기
- **algae** (물속에 사는) 조류
- **hind leg** 뒷다리
- **froglet** 새끼 개구리
- **lose** 잃다

Comprehension Check

A 문장을 읽고 옳으면 T(True), 틀리면 F(False)에 동그라미 하세요.

1 Most frog eggs will hatch. **T / F**

2 The frog eggs become tadpoles after about seven days. **T / F**

3 Six weeks after the hatch, a tadpole looks like a baby frog. **T / F**

B 다음을 읽고 알맞은 답을 고르세요.

1 This passage is mainly about _________________.

ⓐ frog eggs　　　　ⓑ a frog's pond　　　　ⓒ a frog's life cycle

2 How many eggs do frogs lay at one time?

ⓐ About 4,000 eggs

ⓑ Only one egg

ⓒ About 500 eggs

3 What is true about the tadpole nine weeks after it hatches?

ⓐ It becomes a frog.

ⓑ It looks like a baby frog with a tail.

ⓒ It loses its tail.

C 문장을 완성하는 단어를 써 넣으세요.

1 Six weeks after the hatch, a tadpole grows __________ legs and
a __________ tail.

2 A tadpole looks like a baby frog but with a tail. It's called a _________ or
a young frog.

3 At week _________, a froglet loses its tail and becomes an _________
frog.

Read and Understand

● 잘 읽고 이해했나요? 문장의 정확한 의미를 알아보세요.

→ Have you ever seen...?은 경험을 묻는 현재완료 구문으로 '~을 본 적이 있어?'라는 뜻이에요.

1. Have you ever seen / frog eggs / floating in a pond?
________________________   개구리 알들을   연못에 떠 있는

→ up to는 '~까지'라는 뜻이에요.

2. Frogs lay / up to 4,000 eggs / at one time.
개구리들은 낳는다   ________________________   한 번에

3. But / most of them / won't hatch.
그러나   그것들의 대부분은   ________________

→ 조동사 will 뒤에 수동태 be eaten이 연결된 형태예요.

4. Some of the eggs / will be eaten / by other animals, / and other eggs /
알들 중 일부는   ________________   다른 동물들에 의해   그리고 다른 알들은

might dry up / in the sun / or break / in the water.
말라 버릴 수 있다   햇빛에   또는 부서질 수 있다   물속에서

5. The eggs hatch / after about seven days / and the life cycle of tadpoles
알들은 부화한다   ________________________   그리고 올챙이들의 생애주기가 시작된다

begins.

6. A tadpole / begins to swim and eat algae.
올챙이는   ________________________

7. Six weeks after the hatch, / a tadpole grows / hind legs and a longer
________________________   올챙이는 자란다   뒷다리와 더 긴 꼬리가

tail.

8. It eats / tiny insects.
그것은 잡아먹는다   ________________

9. Nine weeks after the hatch, / a tadpole looks like a baby frog /
부화 9주 후에   ________________________

but with a tail.
하지만 꼬리가 있는

10. It's called / a froglet or a young frog.
______________ 새끼 개구리 또는 어린 개구리라고

11. At week sixteen, / a froglet loses its tail / and becomes an adult frog.
16주에 ______________________ 그리고 어른 개구리가 된다

Grammar Point | **will be + 과거분사**

본문 쏙 **Some of the eggs will be eaten by other animals.**
알들 중 일부는 다른 동물들에 의해 먹힐 것이다.

well be eaten은 미래를 나타내는 조동사 will과 수동태 are eaten이 합쳐진 형태예요. 조동사 뒤에는 동사원형이 와야 하므로, will are eaten이 아니라 will be eaten이 된 거예요. 따라서 will be eaten은 '먹힐 것이다'라는 뜻이에요. 이렇게 〈will be + 과거분사〉 형태는 '~될 것이다'라는 미래 수동으로 해석하면 된답니다.

확인문제 **1** The fish will be eaten by the shark.

2 The popcorn will be gone in a minute.

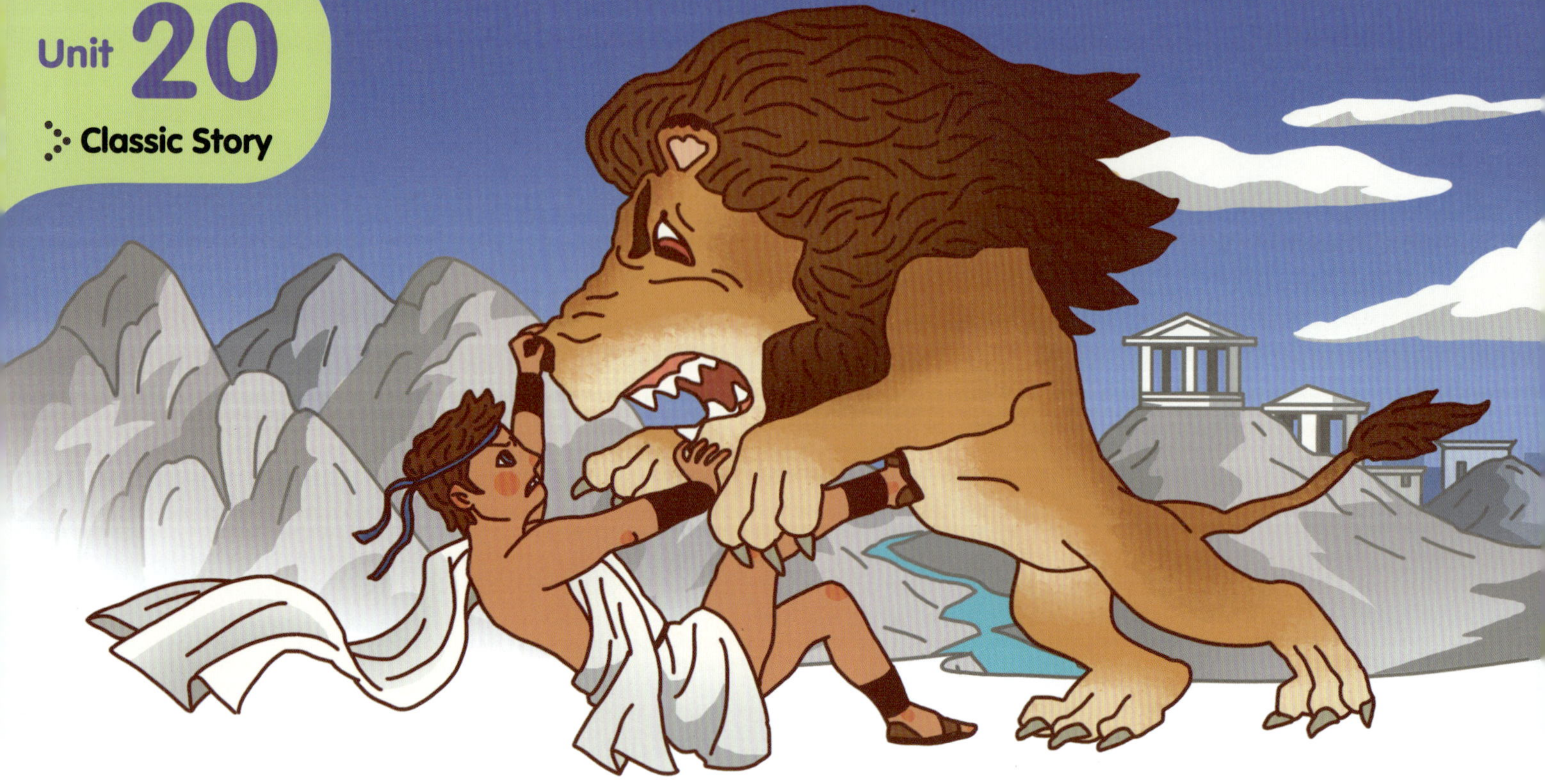

Hercules

Hercules was half man and half god. His father, Zeus, was the king of all the gods, and his mother was a human. But Hercules didn't know that he was part god until he was a grown man.

Zeus's wife, Hera, didn't like Hercules, so she tried all kinds of ways to kill little baby Hercules. She even sent big snakes into his crib. But the strong baby Hercules crushed those snakes. As time passed, he grew into a strong and brave man.

Everyone in the land of Nemea was afraid of the Nemean Lion. It had huge teeth and tough skin that couldn't be pierced by arrows. But Hercules killed the lion, made a coat out of its fur, and wore the lion's head as a helmet. The Nemean Lion was strong, but Hercules was much stronger.

- **half** 절반의
- **grown** 다 큰, 성장한
- **sent** 보냈다 (send 보내다)
- **snake** 뱀
- **crib** 아기 침대
- **crush** 으스러뜨리다
- **brave** 용감한
- **pierce** 뚫다
- **fur** (동물의) 털, 모피
- **wore** 입었다 (wear 입다)
- **helmet** 헬멧, 투구

Comprehension Check

A 문장을 읽고 옳으면 T(True), 틀리면 F(False)에 동그라미 하세요.

1 Hercules was the son of Zeus, the king of all the gods.   **T / F**

2 Hercules's mother was a goddess.   **T / F**

3 Hercules grew into a strong and brave man.   **T / F**

B 다음을 읽고 알맞은 답을 고르세요.

1 This passage is mainly about ________________.

   ⓐ Hercules   ⓑ Zeus   ⓒ Nemean Lion

2 What did Hercules do after he killed the Nemean Lion?

   ⓐ He made a sword and a shield.

   ⓑ He made a coat and a helmet.

   ⓒ He made clothes and shoes.

3 What is true about Hercules?

   ⓐ He crushed the big snakes Hera sent to kill him.

   ⓑ He grew into a weak man.

   ⓒ His father was a human and his mother was a goddess.

C 문장을 완성하는 단어를 써 넣으세요.

1 Hercules didn't know that he was part __________ until he was a __________ man.

2 Hera tried all kinds of __________ to __________ little baby Hercules.

3 The Nemean Lion had huge teeth and __________ skin that couldn't be __________ by arrows.

Read and Understand

● 잘 읽고 이해했나요? 문장의 정확한 의미를 알아보세요.

1. Hercules was / half man and half god.
헤라클레스는 ~였다 _______________

2. His father, Zeus, / was the king of all the gods, / and his mother /
그의 아버지 제우스는 _______________ 그리고 그의 어머니는

was a human.
인간이었다

3. But / Hercules didn't know / that he was part god /
그러나 　헤라클레스는 몰랐다 　그가 일부는 신이라는 것을

→ grown man은 '다 큰 사람', 즉 '성인, 어른'을 뜻해요.

until he was a grown man.
____

여기서 kind는 '종류', way는 '방법'이라는 뜻이에요. ←

4. Zeus's wife, Hera, / didn't like Hercules, / so she tried all kinds of ways /
제우스의 아내, 헤라는 　헤라클레스를 좋아하지 않았다 _______________

to kill little baby Hercules.
어린 아기 헤라클레스를 죽이기 위해

5. She even sent big snakes / into his crib.
_______________ 그의 아기 침대 안으로

6. But / the strong baby Hercules / crushed those snakes.
그러나 　힘센 아기 헤라클레스는 _______________

→ grow into는 '~로 성장하다'라는 뜻이에요.

7. As time passed, / he grew / into a strong and brave man.
_______________ 그는 성장했다 　강하고 용감한 남자로

Nemea는 그리스에 있었던 마을 이름이고,
→ Nemean은 '네메아의, 네메아인'이라는 뜻이에요.

8. Everyone / in the land of Nemea / was afraid of the Nemean Lion.
모든 사람들은 　네메아 땅에 있는 _______________

9. It had / huge teeth and tough skin / that couldn't be pierced by arrows.

그것은 갖고 있었다   커다란 이빨과 단단한 가죽을

10. But Hercules killed the lion, / made a coat out of its fur, /

하지만 헤라클레스는 그 사자를 죽였다

and wore the lion's head / as a helmet.

그리고 사자의 머리를 썼다   투구로

11. The Nemean Lion was strong, / but Hercules was much stronger.

네메아 사자는 강했다

Grammar Point **couldn't be + 과거분사**

본문 쏙 It had huge teeth and tough skin that couldn't be pierced by arrows.

그것은 커다란 이빨과 화살에도 뚫리지 않는 단단한 가죽을 갖고 있었다.

couldn't be pierced는 조동사 couldn't와 수동태 is pierced가 합쳐진 형태예요. 조동사 뒤에는 동사원형이 와야 하므로 couldn't is pierced가 아니라 couldn't be pierced가 된 거예요. 따라서 couldn't be pierced는 '뚫릴 수 없었다'라는 뜻이에요. 이렇게 ⟨couldn't be + 과거분사⟩ 형태는 '~될 수 없었다'라는 과거 수동으로 해석하면 된답니다.

확인문제 **1** The monster couldn't be killed.

2 He said the castle couldn't be destroyed.

Up 7 의문사절을 포함한 5형식 문장 해석하기

누가 한다 무엇이 ~하도록

AI / can even help / doctors / find out / what's wrong with patients.
AI는 심지어 도울 수 있다 의사들을 알아내도록 환자들에게 무엇이 잘못되었는지

해설 AI는 심지어 의사들이 환자에게 어떤 문제가 있는지 찾는 것도 도와줄 수 있어요.

'주어+동사+목적어+목적보어' 구조의 5형식 문장이에요. 이 문장에서 what은 '무엇이' 또는 '어떤 것이'라는 뜻을 가져요. what으로 시작하는 절이 동사 find out의 목적어로 쓰여 '환자들에게 무엇이 잘못되었는지'를 AI가 알아낼 수 있다고 설명하고 있어요.

A 문장을 슬래시(/)로 끊어 읽은 후 우리말 해석을 완성하세요.

1 Teachers can help students learn what they need to know.

→ 교사는 / 도울 수 있다 / 학생들이 / _______________________ / 그들이 알아야 할 것들을

2 I encouraged her to try what she's always wanted to do.

→ 나는 / 격려했다 / 그녀가 / 시도하도록 / _______________________________

3 My mom let me decide what I will eat for dinner.

→ 우리 엄마는 / 하게 한다 / 내가 / 결정하도록 / _______________________________

B 다음 우리말 문장과 일치하도록 영어문장을 알맞게 배열하세요.

1 나는 친구가 파티에 무엇을 입을지를 결정하도록 도왔다.

(helped my friend / what she'll wear for the party / choose / I)

→ ____.

2 경찰은 그녀에게 어젯밤 무엇을 봤는지 설명해 달라고 했다.

(asked / her / the police officer / to explain / what she saw last night)

→ ____.

Up 8   Why don't you 구문 해석하기

동사　　목적어

Why don't you / **try cooking** / **for yourself?**
~하는 게 어때　　　　요리해 보는 게　　　너 스스로를 위해

해설 여러분 스스로를 위해 요리해 보는 건 어때요?

Why don't you는 뒤에 동사원형을 써서 '~해 보는 게 어때?'라고 제안할 때 사용해요. 단어 그대로 '왜 하지 않아요?'라고 해석하지 않아요. 이렇게 자주 쓰이는 표현은 의미를 통째로 기억해 두는 것이 좋아요. try는 '한번 해 보다, 시도하다'라는 의미가 있어, try cooking은 '한번 요리해 보다'로 해석합니다.

A 문장을 슬래시(/)로 끊어 읽은 후 우리말 해석을 완성하세요.

1 Why don't you start a new hobby like painting?

→ ~하는 게 어때 / _______________________ / 그리기와 같은

2 Why don't you come to the party with us?

→ ~하는 게 어때 / _______________________ / 우리와 함께

3 Why don't you focus on your goals?

→ ~하는 게 어때 / _______________________

B 다음 우리말 문장과 일치하도록 영어문장을 알맞게 배열하세요.

1 잠자리에 들기 전에 책을 한 권 읽는 게 어때?

(read a book / why don't you / before going to bed)

→ ____ ?

2 방과 후에 행사에 참석하는 게 어때?

(after school / attend the event / why don't you)

→ ____ ?

Key Words 200

이 책으로 200개 필수 어휘를 마스터 했어!

A

- [ ] **adventure** 모험
- [ ] **alive** 살아 있는
- [ ] **alone** 혼자
- [ ] **amount** 양
- [ ] **ancient** 고대의
- [ ] **Antarctica** 남극 대륙
- [ ] **arrest** 체포하다
- [ ] **artificial** 인공의
- [ ] **atmosphere** (지구의) 대기
- [ ] **attract** 유인하다
- [ ] **aunt** 이모, 고모

B

- [ ] **beg** 간청하다
- [ ] **believe** 믿다
- [ ] **bottle** 병
- [ ] **bow** 절하다
- [ ] **brain** 뇌
- [ ] **brave** 용감한
- [ ] **break** 부서지다
- [ ] **bright** 똑똑한; 밝은
- [ ] **bury** 묻다
- [ ] **busily** 바쁘게

C

- [ ] **calm** 침착한
- [ ] **carpenter** 목수
- [ ] **carve** 조각하다
- [ ] **ceiling** 천장
- [ ] **check** 확인하다
- [ ] **chemical** 화학 물질
- [ ] **chief** 추장, 족장
- [ ] **citizen** 시민, 주민
- [ ] **coast** 해안
- [ ] **company** 회사
- [ ] **conditions** (생활) 환경
- [ ] **confidence** 자신감
- [ ] **construct** 건설하다
- [ ] **continent** 대륙
- [ ] **crawl** 기어가다
- [ ] **creative** 창의적인
- [ ] **crib** 아기 침대
- [ ] **criminal** 범인
- [ ] **crush** 으스러뜨리다
- [ ] **cultural** 문화의

D

- [ ] **decide** 결심하다
- [ ] **dentist** 치과의사
- [ ] **depend on** ~에 의존하다
- [ ] **drugstore** 약국
- [ ] **dry up** 바싹 마르다

E

- [ ] **emotion** 감정
- [ ] **energetic** 활기찬
- [ ] **environment** 환경
- [ ] **errand** 심부름
- [ ] **even** 심지어
- [ ] **evidence** 증거
- [ ] **exact** 정확한
- [ ] **exchange** 교류, 교환
- [ ] **excited** 신이 난
- [ ] **experience** 경험
- [ ] **explain** 설명하다
- [ ] **explore** 탐험하다

F

- [ ] **farming** 농사
- [ ] **fingerprint** 지문
- [ ] **finish** 끝내다
- [ ] **flashlight** 손전등
- [ ] **flesh** 고기, 살
- [ ] **float** (물에) 떠 있다
- [ ] **footprint** 발자국
- [ ] **forget** 잊어버리다
- [ ] **fountain** 분수
- [ ] **fur** (동물의) 털
- [ ] **furniture** 가구

G

- [ ] **garden** 정원
- [ ] **glass** 유리
- [ ] **graveyard** 묘지
- [ ] **greet** 인사하다
- [ ] **grown** 다 큰, 성장한

H

- [ ] **half** 절반의
- [ ] **harbor** 항구
- [ ] **harmony** 조화
- [ ] **harsh** 혹독한
- [ ] **hatch** 부화하다; 부화
- [ ] **healthy** 건강한
- [ ] **heart** (카드의) 하트; 심장
- [ ] **helmet** 헬멧, 투구
- [ ] **hind leg** 뒷다리
- [ ] **history** 역사

- [ ] **hop** 팔짝 뛰다
- [ ] **huge** 거대한

I

- [ ] **immediately** 즉시
- [ ] **improve** 향상시키다
- [ ] **in fact** 사실은
- [ ] **independent** 독립적인
- [ ] **insect** 곤충
- [ ] **intelligence** 지능
- [ ] **island** 섬

L

- [ ] **language** 언어
- [ ] **lawyer** 변호사
- [ ] **lay** (알을) 낳다
- [ ] **leader** 지도자, 대표
- [ ] **life cycle** 생애주기
- [ ] **lose** 잃다
- [ ] **loyalty** 충성

M

- [ ] **mark** 표시하다
- [ ] **mean** 못된
- [ ] **million** 100만
- [ ] **moss** 이끼
- [ ] **musical** 뮤지컬
- [ ] **musty** 퀴퀴한 냄새가 나는
- [ ] **mystery** 미스터리

N

- [ ] **negative** 부정적인
- [ ] **neighbor** 이웃
- [ ] **nervous** 긴장한

O

- [ ] **odor** 악취
- [ ] **order** 주문하다
- [ ] **overcome** 극복하다
- [ ] **own** 고유한

P

- [ ] **paint** 칠하다
- [ ] **patient** 환자
- [ ] **pattern** 무늬, 모양
- [ ] **peace** 평화
- [ ] **pierce** 뚫다
- [ ] **place** 놓다, 두다
- [ ] **plain** 평야
- [ ] **play a role** 역할을 하다
- [ ] **playground** 놀이터
- [ ] **pole** 막대기, 장대
- [ ] **pollinate** 수분하다
- [ ] **pond** 연못
- [ ] **pool** 웅덩이
- [ ] **position** 위치
- [ ] **pretty** 꽤, 매우
- [ ] **prevent** 예방하다
- [ ] **product** 제품
- [ ] **promise** 약속하다
- [ ] **public** 공공의

□ **punishment** 벌, 형벌
□ **puppet** 꼭두각시 인형

Q

□ **queen** 여왕

R

□ **race** 경주하다
□ **realize** 깨닫다
□ **real life** 현실, 실제 생활
□ **recipe** 요리법
□ **recycle** 재활용하다
□ **reduce** 줄이다
□ **relaxed** 편안한
□ **remain** 계속[여전히] ~이다
□ **rescue** 구하다
□ **reside** 거주하다
□ **respect** 존경심; 존경하다
□ **reuse** 재사용하다
□ **rotten** 썩은

S

□ **scent** 향기
□ **science fiction** 공상 과학 소설
□ **scientist** 과학자
□ **scream** 소리를[비명을] 지르다
□ **search** 검색하다
□ **second** 두 번째의
□ **secure** 안심하는

□ **send** 보내다 (과거형 sent)
□ **shelter** 주거지
□ **shore** 해안
□ **sight** 광경, 모습
□ **similar** 비슷한
□ **snail** 달팽이
□ **sound like** ~처럼 들리다
□ **source** 원천, 근원
□ **spend** (시간을) 보내다 (과거형 spent)
□ **statue** 조각상
□ **stink** 악취가 나다
□ **stopwatch** 스톱워치
□ **strange** 낯선, 이상한
□ **successful** 성공한
□ **superhero** 슈퍼히어로
□ **surprised** 놀란
□ **surprising** 놀라운
□ **survive** 살아남다
□ **survivor** 생존자

T

□ **tadpole** 올챙이
□ **take off** 벗다
□ **teenager** 십대
□ **therapist** 치료사
□ **third** 세 번째의
□ **throw away** 버리다
□ **traditional** 전통적인
□ **train** 훈련시키다
□ **translate** 번역하다

U

□ **unique** 독특한
□ **upright** 똑바른, 수직의

W

□ **watch over** 지켜보다
□ **wake up** 깨우다 (과거형 woke up)
□ **welcome** 환영하다
□ **wear** 입다 (과거형 wore)
□ **well-known** 잘 알려진
□ **whenever** ~할 때마다
□ **wig** 가발
□ **wild** 야생의
□ **women** 여자들
□ **wonderland** 이상한 나라
□ **worship** 숭배, 예배
□ **wrap** 감싸다
□ **wreck** 난파선; 난파시키다
□ **write** 쓰다 (과거형 wrote)

MEMO

영어 독해를 완성하는 기적 시리즈

끊어 읽기 연습으로 정확한 독해 완성하기!

기적의 직독직해

끊어 읽는 직독직해 연습으로
영어 이해력, 읽기 속도, 정확성을 동시에 키웁니다.

- 직독직해가 술술 되는 '그래머 포인트'와 '문장 해석법'
- 다양한 장르의 흥미로운 글감을 골고루!
- 단어 연습과 지문 복습을 위한 워크북 제공

전 4권 구성 ｜ 대상: 초등 4~6학년
E2K 지음 ｜ 각 권 168쪽 ｜ 각 권 16,000원 ｜ MP3, 워크시트 5종 다운로드

패턴 문장으로 탄탄한 기초 실력 쌓기!

기적의 패턴리딩

출간 예정
(2025년 2월)

반복 문형이 등장하는 지문 읽기를 통해
어휘와 문형을 자연스럽게 습득합니다.

- 반복 문장 패턴으로 읽기 자신감을 키우는 패턴 리딩
- 다양한 장르의 흥미로운 글감을 골고루!
- 초등 필수 어휘를 확실히 익히는 워크북 제공

전 6권 구성 ｜ 대상: 초등 1~3학년
E2K 지음 ｜ 각 권 140쪽 ｜ 각 권 16,000원 ｜ MP3, 워크시트 4종 다운로드

유아 영어

재미있는 액티비티가 가득한
4~6세를 위한 영어 워크북

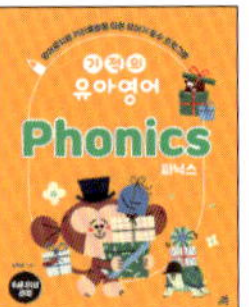

4세 이상	5세 이상	6세 이상	6세 이상

파닉스 완성 프로그램

알파벳 음가 ➡ 사이트 워드
➡ 읽기 연습까지!
리딩을 위한 탄탄한 기초 만들기

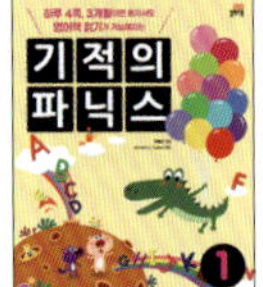

6세 이상 전 3권	1~3학년	1~3학년 전 3권

영어 단어

영어 실력의 가장 큰 바탕은 어휘력!
교과과정 필수 어휘 익히기

1~3학년 전 2권	3학년 이상 전 2권

영어 리딩

패턴 문장 리딩으로 시작해
정확한 해석을 위한 끊어읽기까지!
탄탄한 독해 실력 쌓기

2~3학년 전 3권	3~4학년 전 3권	4~5학년 전 2권	5~6학년 전 2권

영어 라이팅

저학년은 패턴 영작으로,
고학년은 5형식 문장 만들기 연습으로
튼튼한 영작 실력 완성

2학년 이상 전 4권	4학년 이상 전 5권	5학년 이상 전 2권	6학년 이상

영어일기

한 줄 쓰기부터 생활일기,
주제일기까지!
영어 글쓰기 실력을 키우는 시리즈

3학년 이상	4~5학년	5~6학년

영문법

중학 영어 대비, 영어 구사
정확성을 키워주는 영문법 학습

4~5학년 전 2권	5~6학년 전 3권	6학년 이상

기적의 직독직해

120 words B

Workbook & Answers
워크북 및 정답

기적의
직독직해
120 words B

Workbook

Fingerprints

A 우리말 뜻을 쓰고, 영단어를 세 번 쓰면서 철자를 익히세요.

1 fingerprint	지문	fingerprint	fingerprint	fingerprint
2 own				
3 unique				
4 pattern				
5 exact				
6 evidence				
7 criminal				
8 pretty				
9 similar				
10 improve				

B 우리말 뜻에 알맞은 영단어를 연결하세요.

1 범인 •   **ⓐ** exact

2 정확한 •   **ⓑ** fingerprint

3 고유한 •   **ⓒ** criminal

4 지문 •   **ⓓ** improve

5 향상시키다 •   **ⓔ** own

6 무늬, 모양 •   **ⓕ** pattern

7 독특한 •   **ⓖ** pretty

8 증거 •   **ⓗ** evidence

9 비슷한 •   **ⓘ** similar

10 꽤, 매우 •   **ⓙ** unique

C 지문을 다시 읽으며 올바른 단어에 동그라미 하세요.

Fingerprints

Humans have fingerprints on **1**(there / their) fingers. Every finger has its own **2**(same / unique) pattern. No two people in the world have the exact **3**(same / unique) set of lines of fingerprints. Not even identical **4**(brothers / twins) have the same fingerprints. Your fingerprints stay the same from the time you're born **5**(by / until) death. So fingerprints can be used **6**(on / as) evidence to catch criminals.

Humans are not the only ones with fingerprints. Gorillas, chimpanzees, and koala bears have **7**(its / their) own prints. They are pretty similar **8**(to / in) human fingerprints.

So why do we have fingerprints? Fingerprints make the ends of our fingers **9**(smooth / rough). This improves our sense of **10**(smell / touch). Also, rough skin helps us **11**(hold / touch) onto things.

A New Life in America

A 우리말 뜻을 쓰고, 영단어를 세 번 쓰면서 철자를 익히세요.

1 neighbor	이웃	neighbor	neighbor	neighbor
2 greet				
3 welcome				
4 take off				
5 surprising				
6 experience				
7 traditional				
8 explain				
9 cultural				
10 exchange				

B 우리말 뜻에 알맞은 영단어를 연결하세요.

1 이웃 ●   ⓐ cultural

2 문화의 ●   ⓑ take off

3 인사하다 ●   ⓒ neighbor

4 교류 ●   ⓓ greet

5 벗다 ●   ⓔ exchange

6 놀라운 ●   ⓕ experience

7 전통적인 ●   ⓖ surprising

8 설명하다 ●   ⓗ explain

9 환영하다 ●   ⓘ welcome

10 경험 ●   ⓙ traditional

C 지문을 다시 읽으며 올바른 단어에 동그라미 하세요.

A New Life in America

The Kims **1**(emigrated / immigrated) to the United States from South Korea. Ms. Kim made *tteok* to give to her new **2**(friends / neighbors). Mr. Kim, Ms. Kim, Jongmin, and Minhee **3**(ringed / rang) their next-door neighbor's doorbell. Mr. Randy and his family greeted them at the door and **4**(welcome / welcomed) them inside.

The Kims tried to take **5**(of / off) their shoes, but Mr. Randy said that it was okay to wear shoes in his house. It was a **6**(surprised / surprising) experience for the Kims.

The Kims gave *tteok*, a traditional Korean food **7**(who / that) is made of rice and beans, to the Randys. Ms. Kim **8**(invited / explained) that Koreans give *tteok* to their new neighbors when they **9**(meet / move). Ms. Randy thanked her and **10**(invited / explained) them into the kitchen for some homemade apple pie. It was a great cultural **11**(change / exchange).

Pocahontas

A 우리말 뜻을 쓰고, 영단어를 세 번 쓰면서 철자를 익히세요.

1 women	여자들	women	women	women
2 history				
3 chief				
4 strange				
5 leader				
6 beg				
7 rescue				
8 peace				
9 harmony				
10 play a role				

B 우리말 뜻에 알맞은 영단어를 연결하세요.

1 추장　●　　　　ⓐ rescue

2 평화　●　　　　ⓑ chief

3 구하다　●　　　　ⓒ women

4 역사　●　　　　ⓓ peace

5 여자들　●　　　　ⓔ history

6 조화　●　　　　ⓕ play a role

7 낯선, 이상한　●　　　　ⓖ leader

8 역할을 하다　●　　　　ⓗ beg

9 간청하다　●　　　　ⓘ strange

10 지도자　●　　　　ⓙ harmony

C 지문을 다시 읽으며 올바른 단어에 동그라미 하세요.

Pocahontas

Pocahontas is one of the most famous **1**(woman / women) in Native American history. There is a famous story about Pocahontas saving John Smith's **2**(life / role).

Pocahontas was the **3**(wife / daughter) of the chief of the Powhatan people. They were Native **4**(Americas / Americans). When Pocahontas was about twelve years old, strange **5**(Englishman / Englishmen) came to the Powhatans. They wanted to take their **6**(land / food), so the Powhatans and the Englishmen fought.

One day, the leader of the Englishmen, John Smith, **7**(caught / was caught) and the chief of the Powhatans was **8**(around / about) to kill him. Pocahontas **9**(begged / rescued) her father not to kill the man and she **10**(begged / rescued) him. She wanted both of them to live in **11**(peace / piece) and harmony. Pocahontas played an important **12**(life / role) between the Native Americans and the Englishmen.

A　우리말 뜻을 쓰고, 영단어를 세 번 쓰면서 철자를 익히세요.

1 carpenter	목수	carpenter	carpenter	carpenter
2 puppet				
3 carve				
4 surprised				
5 alive				
6 remain				
7 finish				
8 wig				
9 scream				
10 forget				

B　우리말 뜻에 알맞은 영단어를 연결하세요.

1 꼭두각시 인형 ●　　ⓐ wig

2 끝내다 ●　　ⓑ carve

3 살아 있는 ●　　ⓒ finish

4 조각하다 ●　　ⓓ alive

5 가발 ●　　ⓔ puppet

6 잊어버리다 ●　　ⓕ surprised

7 계속 ~이다 ●　　ⓖ scream

8 목수 ●　　ⓗ forget

9 소리를 지르다 ●　　ⓘ remain

10 놀란 ●　　ⓙ carpenter

C 지문을 다시 읽으며 올바른 단어에 동그라미 하세요.

Pinocchio

Once upon a time, a carpenter found a **1**(talk / talking) piece of wood and he gave it to his friend, Geppetto. Geppetto wanted to make a **2**(robot / puppet), so he took it home. He would call the puppet Pinocchio.

When he started to **3**(cut / carve) the wood, a voice **4**(screamed / squealed). "Ouch! That hurt!" Geppetto was **5**(surprising / surprised) to find that the wood was **6**(live / alive). He carved a head, hair, eyes, and a nose. When he carved out the nose, it grew **7**(shorter and shorter / longer and longer). Geppetto cut it down, but it **8**(returned / remained) a long nose.

When Geppetto was almost finished **9**(to make / making) Pinocchio, it took Geppetto's **10**(hat / wig) off and ran away from the house. "You naughty boy! Come back!" Geppetto **11**(screamed / squealed), but Pinocchio couldn't hear because Geppetto **12**(forgot / had forgotten) to carve the ears.

Flower Scents

A 우리말 뜻을 쓰고, 영단어를 세 번 쓰면서 철자를 익히세요.

		향기	scent	scent	scent
1	scent				
2	in fact				
3	stink				
4	rotten				
5	flesh				
6	attract				
7	pollinate				
8	chemical				
9	insect				
10	odor				

B 우리말 뜻에 알맞은 영단어를 연결하세요.

1 향기 ●	ⓐ odor	
2 화학 물질 ●	ⓑ scent	
3 악취 ●	ⓒ chemical	
4 고기, 살 ●	ⓓ pollinate	
5 수분하다 ●	ⓔ flesh	
6 유인하다 ●	ⓕ rotten	
7 곤충 ●	ⓖ stink	
8 사실은 ●	ⓗ insect	
9 썩은 ●	ⓘ attract	
10 악취가 나다 ●	ⓙ in fact	

C 지문을 다시 읽으며 올바른 단어에 동그라미 하세요.

Flower Scents

When most people think of flowers, they think of sweet **1**(scents / odors). But this is not **2**(almost / always) the case. Not all flowers smell sweet. **3**(On / In) fact, some flowers **4**(stink / smell). A huge flower in Sumatra, the titan arum, smells like **5**(roten / rotten) flesh. This smell attracts flies **6**(as that / so that) the flower can be pollinated.

Why do flowers have scents? There should be a **7**(answer / reason). Flowers make **8**(chemicals / pollinators) to attract insects or birds. They will visit and pollinate flowers.

Flowers have different smells because they attract different **9**(chemicals / pollinators). Flowers pollinated **10**(of / by) bees and butterflies have sweet scents. Flowers **11**(pollinating / pollinated) by moths have stronger scents at night than during the day. Flowers pollinated by bats have musty **12**(scents / odors). Flowers pollinated by beetles have fruity scents.

Exploring a Cave

A 우리말 뜻을 쓰고, 영단어를 세 번 쓰면서 철자를 익히세요.

1	explore	탐험하다	explore	explore	explore
2	excited				
3	nervous				
4	moss				
5	snail				
6	crawl				
7	hop				
8	flashlight				
9	ceiling				
10	pool				

B 우리말 뜻에 알맞은 영단어를 연결하세요.

1 신이 난 ●	ⓐ snail		6 탐험하다 ●	ⓕ moss
2 웅덩이 ●	ⓑ pool		7 이끼 ●	ⓖ crawl
3 천장 ●	ⓒ nervous		8 기어가다 ●	ⓗ explore
4 달팽이 ●	ⓓ excited		9 팔짝 뛰다 ●	ⓘ hop
5 긴장한 ●	ⓔ ceiling		10 손전등 ●	ⓙ flashlight

C 지문을 다시 읽으며 올바른 단어에 동그라미 하세요.

Exploring a Cave

Today our class went on a field **1**(trip / travel) to explore a cave. We were all **2**(exciting / excited) and nervous about going into the cave.

When we entered the cave, we saw moss **3**(growing / crawling) on stones and some spider webs. When we passed some white snails **4**(growing / crawling) on the moss, something hopped in front of us. All the students **5**(laughed / screamed). It was just a frog. We didn't know that frogs lived in caves.

We kept **6**(to walk / walking) deeper into the cave. There was some **7**(moving / movement) on the wall. The teacher **8**(shined / shone) the flashlight and we saw lizards. Then on the **9**(ceiling / floor) we saw bats **10**(folding / spreading) their wings. **11**(First / Finally), we saw a crayfish in a **12**(river / pool) of water in the cave. We didn't know that so many different animals lived in caves.

Reduce, Reuse, and Recycle

A 우리말 뜻을 쓰고, 영단어를 세 번 쓰면서 철자를 익히세요.

1	environment	환경	environment	environment	environment
2	reduce				
3	reuse				
4	recycle				
5	throw away				
6	glass				
7	bottle				
8	million				
9	amount				
10	product				

B 우리말 뜻에 알맞은 영단어를 연결하세요.

1 병	•	ⓐ product	6 줄이다	•	ⓕ throw away
2 제품	•	ⓑ bottle	7 버리다	•	ⓖ reduce
3 100만	•	ⓒ amount	8 유리	•	ⓗ recycle
4 재사용하다	•	ⓓ million	9 재활용하다	•	ⓘ environment
5 양	•	ⓔ reuse	10 환경	•	ⓙ glass

C 지문을 다시 읽으며 올바른 단어에 동그라미 하세요.

Reduce, Reuse, and Recycle

It's time to **1**(learn / teach) the three R's of the environment: reduce, reuse, and recycle. Every year, Americans **2**(take / throw) away 27 billion glass bottles, 35 million tons of food, and 65 million plastic and metal cans. Where does all of this waste go? It all **3**(recycles / remains) in the land and **4**(makes / takes) from 100 to 4,000 years to decompose.

The best **5**(time / way) to help the environment is to **6**(reduce / produce) the amount of waste we **7**(reduce / produce). We should buy products that **8**(have / don't have) a lot of packaging. Another way to help the environment is to **9**(reuse / reduce) things instead of throwing them **10**(off / away). Lastly, **11**(reduce / recycle) things to create new products out of the materials from the old ones. We should also look for products that **12**(produce / contain) recycled materials.

A 우리말 뜻을 쓰고, 영단어를 세 번 쓰면서 철자를 익히세요.

1 garden	정원	garden	garden	garden
2 busily				
3 paint				
4 queen				
5 heart				
6 check				
7 woke up				
8 realize				
9 adventure				
10 wonderland				

B 우리말 뜻에 알맞은 영단어를 연결하세요.

1 칠하다 ●   ⓐ busily

2 여왕 ●   ⓑ wonderland

3 바쁘게 ●   ⓒ paint

4 이상한 나라 ●   ⓓ adventure

5 모험 ●   ⓔ queen

6 확인하다 ●   ⓕ heart

7 하트 ●   ⓖ garden

8 정원 ●   ⓗ woke up

9 깨닫다 ●   ⓘ realize

10 깨웠다 ●   ⓙ check

C 지문을 다시 읽으며 올바른 단어에 동그라미 하세요.

Alice's Adventures in Wonderland

Alice saw white roses **1**(growing / painting) in a garden. Three playing cards were **2**(busy / busily) painting some white roses red. Alice was **3**(curious / angry) about this.

"**4**(How / Why) are you painting the white roses red?" asked Alice.

"The Queen of Hearts wants all roses **5**(be / to be) red," the Five of Spades answered.

6(Than / Then) the Queen of Hearts and the playing card soldiers came to the garden. The Queen **7**(realized / checked) the roses and said to the playing card soldiers, "**8**(Of / Off) with their heads!"

Alice was angry. "No, you can't do that!" said Alice.

"Yes, I can! Off with your **9**(head / hair), too," said the Queen.

"No, no, no!" said Alice.

Suddenly, Alice's sister **10**(waked / woke) Alice up. Alice **11**(realized / checked) it was just a **12**(exciting / strange) dream. It was Alice's adventures in Wonderland!

Unit 9   A Pioneer in Tech Industry

A 우리말 뜻을 쓰고, 영단어를 세 번 쓰면서 철자를 익히세요.

1	programmer	프로그래머	programmer	programmer	programmer
2	company				
3	successful				
4	lawyer				
5	bright				
6	wrote				
7	teenager				
8	enter				
9	spent				
10	confidence				

B 우리말 뜻에 알맞은 영단어를 연결하세요.

1 썼다	ⓐ confidence	6 입학하다	ⓕ lawyer
2 프로그래머	ⓑ successful	7 변호사	ⓖ teenager
3 자신감	ⓒ wrote	8 (시간을) 보냈다	ⓗ company
4 성공한	ⓓ bright	9 회사	ⓘ spent
5 똑똑한	ⓔ programmer	10 십대	ⓙ enter

C 지문을 다시 읽으며 올바른 단어에 동그라미 하세요.

A Pioneer in Tech Industry

Bill Gates is an American computer programmer **1**(who / which) is the co-founder of Microsoft, one of the **2**(larger / largest) PC software companies in the world. His work with computers has made a **3**(small / big) difference around the world.

Bill was born **4**(as / on) the son of a **5**(successful / succeed) lawyer in 1955. Young Bill was a **6**(bright / light) and curious boy. He **7**(writed / wrote) his first computer program as a young teenager. Bill **8**(entered / dropped) Harvard University to study law, but he **9**(spended / spent) most of his time on computers. In 1975, he **10**(attended / dropped) out of Harvard to start a software company with his friend Paul Allen. That company was Microsoft.

Bill Gates wasn't afraid to take **11**(company / risks). He had **12**(confident / confidence) in himself and his products.

Visiting New York

A 우리말 뜻을 쓰고, 영단어를 세 번 쓰면서 철자를 익히세요.

1 aunt	이모, 고모	aunt	aunt	aunt
2 public				
3 huge				
4 fountain				
5 second				
6 statue				
7 island				
8 harbor				
9 third				
10 musical				

B 우리말 뜻에 알맞은 영단어를 연결하세요.

1 거대한 ●		❶ aunt
2 이모, 고모 ●		❷ public
3 공공의 ●		❸ fountain
4 분수 ●		❹ second
5 두 번째의 ●		❺ huge

6 조각상 ●		❻ island
7 뮤지컬 ●		❼ statue
8 항구 ●		❽ harbor
9 세 번째의 ●		❾ musical
10 섬 ●		❿ third

C 지문을 다시 읽으며 올바른 단어에 동그라미 하세요.

Visiting New York

My brother Kevin and I visited Aunt Ann, **1**(who / which) lives in New York City. This was our **2**(first / second) visit to New York, so we wanted to see many **3**(statues / landmarks).

On the first day, we **4**(taked / took) a bus and went to Central Park. It is a public park **5**(who / which) is located in Manhattan. It is huge, and we saw lakes, fountains, and bridges.

On the **6**(two / second) day, we took a ferry to **7**(climb / visit) the Statue of Liberty. It is a huge statue on Liberty Island in New York **8**(Island / Harbor). We went to the **9**(top / bottom) of the statue in an elevator.

On the **10**(three / third) day, we took a taxi and went to New York Times Square. We **11**(saw / looked) many people and buildings. We **12**(watched / saw) a famous musical. We had lots of fun with Aunt Ann.

Icy Land: Antarctica

A 우리말 뜻을 쓰고, 영단어를 세 번 쓰면서 철자를 익히세요.

1	Antarctica	남극 대륙 Antarctica	Antarctica	Antarctica
2	continent			
3	reside			
4	harsh			
5	conditions			
6	scientist			
7	atmosphere			
8	well-known			
9	depend on			
10	source			

B 우리말 뜻에 알맞은 영단어를 연결하세요.

1 거주하다 ●	ⓐ well-known	6 혹독한 ●	ⓕ scientist
2 잘 알려진 ●	ⓑ Antarctica	7 과학자 ●	ⓖ harsh
3 남극 대륙 ●	ⓒ conditions	8 원천, 근원 ●	ⓗ atmosphere
4 ~에 의존하다 ●	ⓓ reside	9 (지구의) 대기 ●	ⓘ source
5 (생활) 환경 ●	ⓔ depend on	10 대륙 ●	ⓙ continent

C 지문을 다시 읽으며 올바른 단어에 동그라미 하세요.

Icy Land: Antarctica

Antarctica is the southernmost **1**(sea / continent) on the earth, and the South Pole **2**(finds / is found) there. Most of Antarctica **3**(covers / is covered) in ice, and it has almost 90% of all the world's ice.

Antarctica is the **4**(hottest / coldest) continent on the earth. The average summer **5**(temperature / atmosphere) is −27.5℃, and the average winter temperature is −60℃. People don't permanently **6**(reside / depend) in Antarctica **7**(because / because of) the harsh living conditions. Most people **8**(who / which) live there are scientists. They study the weather, animals, glaciers, and the earth's atmosphere.

There are **9**(well-know / well-known) animals that live in Antarctica. Whales, penguins, and seals live there. They **10**(most / mostly) depend **11**(in / on) krill, so krill are an important source of food in Antarctica.

William Tell

A 우리말 뜻을 쓰고, 영단어를 세 번 쓰면서 철자를 익히세요.

1 mean	못된	mean	mean	mean
2 loyalty				
3 citizen				
4 pole				
5 bow				
6 respect				
7 immediately				
8 arrest				
9 punishment				
10 place				

B 우리말 뜻에 알맞은 영단어를 연결하세요.

1 충성 • **ⓐ** arrest

2 체포하다 • **ⓑ** pole

3 못된 • **ⓒ** bow

4 막대기, 장대 • **ⓓ** loyalty

5 절하다 • **ⓔ** mean

6 존경심 • **ⓕ** immediately

7 놓다, 두다 • **ⓖ** punishment

8 시민, 주민 • **ⓗ** respect

9 벌, 형벌 • **ⓘ** place

10 즉시 • **ⓙ** citizen

C   지문을 다시 읽으며 올바른 단어에 동그라미 하세요.

William Tell

Baron Gessler was a mean governor **1**(who / which) wanted to test the **2**(royalty / loyalty) of the citizens. To do so, he had his hat **3**(hang / hung) on a pole and everyone passing **4**(have to / had to) bow to the hat in order to show their respect.

One day, William Tell passed the hat with his young son, Carl. But he didn't bow to the hat. Immediately, he **5**(arrested / was arrested). As punishment, Gessler told Tell to **6**(shoot / shot) an apple on his son's head. Tell's son was placed **7**(again / against) a tree, and an apple **8**(put / was put) on his head.

Tell took two arrows out, and **9**(shoot / shot) one arrow at his son. It went **10**(away / through) the apple. Gessler asked Tell **11**(why / what) he had another arrow. Tell told Gessler that **12**(because / if) the first arrow killed his son, he was going to shoot the second arrow into Gessler's heart.

Color Therapy

A 우리말 뜻을 쓰고, 영단어를 세 번 쓰면서 철자를 익히세요.

1 emotion	감정	emotion	emotion	emotion
2 dentist				
3 patient				
4 calm				
5 secure				
6 overcome				
7 negative				
8 wrap				
9 energetic				
10 relaxed				

B 우리말 뜻에 알맞은 영단어를 연결하세요.

1 치과의사 ●	ⓐ relaxed	6 환자 ●	ⓕ negative
2 편안한 ●	ⓑ emotion	7 침착한 ●	ⓖ energetic
3 감정 ●	ⓒ overcome	8 부정적인 ●	ⓗ calm
4 극복하다 ●	ⓓ dentist	9 활기찬 ●	ⓘ wrap
5 안심하는 ●	ⓔ secure	10 감싸다 ●	ⓙ patient

C 지문을 다시 읽으며 올바른 단어에 동그라미 하세요.

Color Therapy

How do you feel **1**(what / when) you see the color red? Do you feel angry? How about blue? Does it make you feel **2**(stupid / smart)? Different colors make you feel different **3**(emotions / therapy). When colors are used to make people feel a **4**(certain / certainly) way, this is called "color therapy."

You probably don't like to go to the dentist's office. Who does? Dentists use color **5**(therapist / therapy) to make their patients feel better. They might paint the walls **6**(blue / green) or yellow. Green makes the patients feel calm and **7**(sad / secure). Yellow helps the patients feel **8**(bright / angry) and cheery.

Some **9**(therapists / therapy) use colors to help people overcome **10**(positive / negative) emotions. They shine colored lights on patients, or **11**(rap / wrap) their bodies in colored silks. They try to make the patients feel happier, **12**(energeticer / more energetic), or more relaxed.

Nick, the Superhero

A 우리말 뜻을 쓰고, 영단어를 세 번 쓰면서 철자를 익히세요.

1	superhero	슈퍼히어로	superhero	superhero	superhero
2	whenever				
3	errand				
4	stopwatch				
5	furniture				
6	race				
7	playground				
8	watch over				
9	believe				
10	train				

B 우리말 뜻에 알맞은 영단어를 연결하세요.

1 심부름   •   **ⓐ** furniture

2 가구   •   **ⓑ** errand

3 믿다   •   **ⓒ** race

4 ~할 때마다 •   **ⓓ** believe

5 경주하다   •   **ⓔ** whenever

6 스톱워치   •   **ⓕ** superhero

7 슈퍼히어로 •   **ⓖ** stopwatch

8 훈련시키다 •   **ⓗ** watch over

9 지켜보다   •   **ⓘ** playground

10 놀이터   •   **ⓙ** train

C 지문을 다시 읽으며 올바른 단어에 동그라미 하세요.

Nick, the Superhero

Nick loved to read superhero stories. He always wanted to be **1**(as / like) a superhero. **2**(However / Whenever) he did something, he did it like a superhero.

When he **3**(walked / ran) an errand for his mother, he ran as **4**(fast / faster) as he could. When he did his homework, he **5**(trained / timed) himself with a stopwatch. When he **6**(washed / cleaned) up his room, he moved all of the **7**(furniture / furnitures) single-handedly. When he **8**(rided / rode) his bike to school, he raced **9**(to / against) the school bus. When he went to the playground, he didn't play with his friends. He went up to the top of the jungle gym and watched **10**(out / over) the other kids.

Nick believed that someday he could help **11**(anothers / others) like a superhero. This is why he **12**(trained / timed) himself all the time.

Stonehenge

A 우리말 뜻을 쓰고, 영단어를 세 번 쓰면서 철자를 익히세요.

1 ancient	고대의	ancient	ancient	ancient
2 mystery				
3 sight				
4 plain				
5 upright				
6 bury				
7 mark				
8 position				
9 graveyard				
10 worship				

B 우리말 뜻에 알맞은 영단어를 연결하세요.

1 평야 •   **ⓐ** upright   **6** 고대의 •   **ⓕ** mystery

2 숭배, 예배 •   **ⓑ** sight   **7** 표시하다 •   **ⓖ** position

3 똑바른, 수직의 •   **ⓒ** plain   **8** 위치 •   **ⓗ** ancient

4 묻다 •   **ⓓ** worship   **9** 미스터리 •   **ⓘ** graveyard

5 광경, 모습 •   **ⓔ** bury   **10** 묘지 •   **ⓙ** mark

C 지문을 다시 읽으며 올바른 단어에 동그라미 하세요.

Stonehenge

Stonehenge, like the pyramids of Egypt, is an ancient **1**(story / mystery) of the world. It is a very strange **2**(site / sight). On a green wide-open plain, huge **3**(circle / rectangular) stones stand upright, almost 9 meters tall. Other stones are **4**(built / placed) on top of them. Who put those stones there? And why?

We may never know **5**(exact / exactly) why. Part of the reason is that different groups built Stonehenge **6**(over / on) 700 years! First, people buried their **7**(die / dead) around the circle that they **8**(digged / dug) into the ground. Later, people put **9**(metal / wooden) poles in a circle to mark the positions of the sun, moon, and stars. Finally, stones were placed in a **10**(circle / rentangle). Stonehenge started as a **11**(worship / graveyard). Later it became a place of **12**(worship / graveyard) and mystery.

Robinson Crusoe

A 우리말 뜻을 쓰고, 영단어를 세 번 쓰면서 철자를 익히세요.

1 coast	해안	coast	coast	coast
2 survive				
3 shore				
4 survivor				
5 wreck				
6 shelter				
7 wild				
8 construct				
9 farming				
10 footprint				

B 우리말 뜻에 알맞은 영단어를 연결하세요.

1 해안 ●	ⓐ survivor	**6** 해안 ●	ⓕ wreck
2 발자국 ●	ⓑ shore	**7** 농사 ●	ⓖ shelter
3 생존자 ●	ⓒ survive	**8** 난파선 ●	ⓗ coast
4 살아남다 ●	ⓓ footprint	**9** 주거지 ●	ⓘ wild
5 건설하다 ●	ⓔ construct	**10** 야생의 ●	ⓙ farming

C 지문을 다시 읽으며 올바른 단어에 동그라미 하세요.

Robinson Crusoe

Robinson Crusoe was shipwrecked **1**(of / off) the coast of South America. He **2**(survivor / survived) a huge storm and was washed up on the shore of an island. He knew that he was the only **3**(survivor / survived) of the wreck.

Crusoe wanted to live, so he planned how to get food and shelter to **4**(protect / construct) himself from wild animals. He searched the **5**(washed / wrecked) ship and collected food and useful items. He **6**(found / finded) some biscuits, some dried meat, some alcohol, a spyglass, axes, and some guns.

7(On / As) time passed, Crusoe **8**(learned / constructed) many useful things like a canoe and houses. He also learned about **9**(farming / farmer). After **10**(spend / spending) about fifteen years on the island, he found a man's **11**(fingerprints / footprints). There were **12**(man / men) living on the island. Who could they be?

Understanding AI

A 우리말 뜻을 쓰고, 영단어를 세 번 쓰면서 철자를 익히세요.

1	artificial	인공의	artificial	artificial	artificial
2	intelligence				
3	even				
4	patient				
5	translate				
6	language				
7	brain				
8	sound like				
9	science fiction				
10	real life				

B 우리말 뜻에 알맞은 영단어를 연결하세요.

1 공상 과학 소설 ●	ⓐ language
2 뇌 ●	ⓑ artificial
3 언어 ●	ⓒ brain
4 심지어 ●	ⓓ science fiction
5 인공의 ●	ⓔ even
6 ~처럼 들리다 ●	ⓕ patient
7 현실 ●	ⓖ translate
8 지능 ●	ⓗ sound like
9 번역하다 ●	ⓘ real life
10 환자 ●	ⓙ intelligence

C 지문을 다시 읽으며 올바른 단어에 동그라미 하세요.

Understanding AI

AI, **1**(and / or) Artificial Intelligence, is like a smart computer that can learn and think. It's used in many things we see **2**(every day / everyday).

For example, **3**(when / where) you talk to Siri or Alexa, that's AI **4**(helped / helping) you. AI can play games, answer questions, and **5**(even / with) help doctors find out what's wrong with patients. It can **6**(so / also) translate languages, so you can talk to someone who speaks a different language. Think of it **7**(as / at) a robot brain that **8**(help / helps) people do things faster and **9**(good / better). In schools, AI can help you learn **10**(for / by) giving you fun quizzes and games.

While it **11**(might / will) sound like science fiction, AI is here to help us **12**(in / on) real life, making our lives easier and more fun.

Cooking for Myself

A 우리말 뜻을 쓰고, 영단어를 세 번 쓰면서 철자를 익히세요.

1 drugstore	약국	drugstore	drugstore	drugstore
2 alone				
3 order				
4 prevent				
5 healthy				
6 creative				
7 independent				
8 decide				
9 promise				
10 search				

B 우리말 뜻에 알맞은 영단어를 연결하세요.

1 혼자 •   ⓐ order

2 창의적인 •   ⓑ creative

3 검색하다 •   ⓒ drugstore

4 약국 •   ⓓ alone

5 주문하다 •   ⓔ search

6 독립적인 •   ⓕ promise

7 결심하다 •   ⓖ independent

8 약속하다 •   ⓗ prevent

9 예방하다 •   ⓘ healthy

10 건강한 •   ⓙ decide

C 지문을 다시 읽으며 올바른 단어에 동그라미 하세요.

Cooking for Myself

I'm Ryan. I'm a junior high school student. My parents **1**(walk / run) a drugstore, so they need to work until late at night. Since I'm an **2**(unique / only) child, I often eat dinner alone. My parents let me **3**(order / to order) pizza or pick up a hamburger from a fast-food place. But now I have gotten tired of **4**(eat / eating) fast food for dinner all the time.

I learned at school that **5**(cook / cooking) food for yourself is important. It can **6**(provide / prevent) obesity and keep you **7**(health / healthy). It can also make you **8**(careful / creative) and independent. Therefore, I've decided to cook food for myself. Of course I promised my parents that I would be **9**(careful / creative) with the stove and **10**(knifes / knives).

I **11**(looked / searched) the Internet and found some simple recipes. For starters, I'm going to cook an omelet. Why don't you try **12**(to cook / cooking) for yourself?

A   우리말 뜻을 쓰고, 영단어를 세 번 쓰면서 철자를 익히세요.

1	float	(물에) 떠 있다	float	float	float
2	pond				
3	lay				
4	hatch				
5	dry up				
6	break				
7	tadpole				
8	life cycle				
9	hind leg				
10	lose				

B   우리말 뜻에 알맞은 영단어를 연결하세요.

1 연못 •	ⓐ hind leg
2 (알을) 낳다 •	ⓑ pond
3 뒷다리 •	ⓒ lose
4 올챙이 •	ⓓ lay
5 잃다 •	ⓔ tadpole
6 생애주기 •	ⓕ float
7 부서지다 •	ⓖ break
8 바싹 마르다 •	ⓗ dry up
9 (물에) 떠 있다 •	ⓘ hatch
10 부화하다 •	ⓙ life cycle

C 지문을 다시 읽으며 올바른 단어에 동그라미 하세요.

Frogs

Have you ever **1**(saw / seen) frog eggs **2**(floating / floated) in a pond? Frogs **3**(lie / lay) up to 4,000 eggs at one time. But most of them won't **4**(break / hatch). Some of the eggs will **5**(are / be) eaten by other animals, and other eggs might dry up in the sun or break in the water.

The eggs hatch after about seven days and the life cycle of **6**(froglets / tadpoles) begins. A tadpole begins to swim and eat algae. Six weeks after the hatch, a tadpole grows **7**(front / hind) legs and a longer tail. It eats **8**(large / tiny) insects.

Nine weeks after the hatch, a tadpole looks like a baby frog but **9**(with / without) a tail. It's called a **10**(froglet / tadpole) or a young frog. At week sixteen, a froglet **11**(grows / loses) its tail and becomes an **12**(young / adult) frog.

A 우리말 뜻을 쓰고, 영단어를 세 번 쓰면서 철자를 익히세요.

1 half	절반의	half	half	half
2 grown				
3 sent				
4 crib				
5 crush				
6 brave				
7 pierce				
8 fur				
9 wore				
10 helmet				

B 우리말 뜻에 알맞은 영단어를 연결하세요.

1 용감한 •	ⓐ grown	6 아기 침대 •	ⓕ pierce
2 (동물의) 털 •	ⓑ wore	7 뚫다 •	ⓖ crib
3 입었다 •	ⓒ brave	8 으스러뜨리다 •	ⓗ sent
4 헬멧, 투구 •	ⓓ fur	9 절반의 •	ⓘ half
5 다 큰 •	ⓔ helmet	10 보냈다 •	ⓙ crush

C 지문을 다시 읽으며 올바른 단어에 동그라미 하세요.

Hercules

Hercules was half man and half **1**(god / goddess). His father, Zeus, was the king of all the gods, and his mother was a **2**(goddess / human). But Hercules didn't know that he was part god until he was a **3**(grew / grown) man.

Zeus's wife, Hera, didn't like Hercules, so she tried all **4**(kind / kinds) of ways to kill little baby Hercules. She even **5**(sended / sent) big snakes into his crib. But the strong baby Hercules **6**(crushed / crashed) those snakes. As time passed, he **7**(grew / grown) into a strong and brave man.

Everyone in the land of Nemea was afraid **8**(in / of) the Nemean Lion. It had huge teeth and tough skin that couldn't **9**(is / be) pierced by arrows. But Hercules killed the lion, made a coat **10**(from / out of) its fur, and **11**(weared / wore) the lion's head as a helmet. The Nemean Lion was strong, but Hercules was much **12**(stronger / strongest).

기적의 직독직해

120 words B

Answers

사람은 손가락에 지문이 있어요. 모든 손가락에는 그것 고유의 독특한 무늬가 있어요. 세상의 어떤 두 사람도 지문의 선 세트가 정확히 똑같지는 않아요. 심지어 일란성 쌍둥이도 똑같은 지문을 가지고 있지 않아요. 여러분의 지문은 여러분이 태어날 때부터 죽을 때까지 같은 모양을 유지해요. 그래서 지문은 범인을 잡는 증거로 사용될 수 있어요.

사람만 지문이 있는 것은 아니에요. 고릴라, 침팬지, 그리고 코알라도 그들 고유의 지문이 있어요. 그 지문들은 사람의 지문과 꽤 비슷해요.

그러면 우리는 왜 지문을 가지고 있는 걸까요? 지문은 우리의 손가락 끝을 거칠게 만들어요. 이것은 우리의 촉각을 향상시켜요. 또한 거친 피부는 우리가 물건을 잡는 데 도움을 줘요.

Comprehension Check   13쪽

A 1. F 오직 사람만 손가락에 지문이 있어요.
   2. F 일란성 쌍둥이는 똑같은 지문을 가지고 있어요.
   3. T 코알라는 그들 고유의 지문이 있어요.

B 1. ⓑ 이 지문은 주로 지문에 대한 거예요.
     ⓐ 사람의 손가락들   ⓒ 발자국들
   2. ⓐ 지문이 어떻게 우리들을 돕나요?
     ⓐ 지문은 우리가 물건을 잡을 수 있게 해요.
     ⓑ 지문은 우리가 물건 냄새를 맡을 수 있게 해요.
     ⓒ 지문은 우리가 손뼉칠 수 있게 해요.
   3. ⓑ 지문을 가지고 있지 않은 것은 무엇인가요?
     ⓐ 코알라   ⓑ 상어   ⓒ 사람

C 1. pattern 모든 손가락에는 그것 고유의 독특한 무늬가 있어요.
   2. exact, lines 세상의 어떤 두 사람도 지문의 선 세트가 정확히 똑같지는 않아요.
   3. born, death 여러분의 지문은 여러분이 태어날 때부터 죽을 때까지 같은 모양을 유지해요.

Read and Understand   14쪽

1. 그들의 손가락에
2. 그것 고유의 독특한 무늬를
3. 세상의 어떤 두 사람도 가지고 있지 않다
4. 심지어 일란성 쌍둥이도 가지고 있지 않다
5. 여러분의 지문은 같은 모양을 유지한다
6. 범인들을 잡는
7. 지문을 가진
8. 그들 고유의 지문을 가지고 있다
9. 그것들은 꽤 비슷하다
10. 우리는 왜 가지고 있을까?
11. 우리의 손가락 끝을
12. 우리의 촉각을
13. 우리가 물건을 잡는 것을

Grammar Point   15쪽

1. 심지어 우리 선생님도 결과를 모른다.
2. 심지어 제인도 내 이름을 기억하지 못했다.

Workbook

A
1. 지문
2. 고유한
3. 독특한
4. 무늬, 모양
5. 정확한
6. 증거
7. 범인
8. 꽤, 매우
9. 비슷한
10. 향상시키다

B
1. ⓒ
2. ⓐ
3. ⓔ
4. ⓑ
5. ⓓ
6. ⓕ
7. ⓙ
8. ⓗ
9. ⓘ
10. ⓖ

C
1. their
2. unique
3. same
4. twins
5. until
6. as
7. their
8. to
9. rough
10. touch
11. hold

A New Life in America | 미국에서의 새로운 생활

김씨네 가족은 한국에서 미국으로 이민을 왔어요. 김씨 아주머니는 새로운 이웃들에게 줄 떡을 만들었어요. 김씨 아저씨, 김씨 아주머니, 종민, 그리고 민희는 옆집 이웃의 초인종을 눌렀어요. 랜디씨와 그의 가족이 문 앞에서 그들에게 인사했고, 그들을 환영하며 안으로 맞이했어요.

김씨네 가족은 신발을 벗으려 했지만 랜디씨가 그의 집에서는 신발을 신고 있어도 괜찮다고 말했어요. 이것은 김씨네 가족에게 놀라운 경험이었어요.

김씨네 가족은 쌀과 팥으로 만든 한국의 전통 음식인 떡을 랜디씨 가족에게 줬어요. 김씨 아주머니는 한국인들은 이사를 하면 새로운 이웃에게 떡을 준다고 설명했어요. 랜디 아주머니는 고마워하며 집에서 만든 애플파이를 주기 위해 그들을 부엌으로 안내했어요. 이것은 훌륭한 문화 교류였어요.

Comprehension Check 17쪽

A 1. F 김씨네 가족은 미국에서 한국으로 이사했어요.
2. T 김씨네 가족은 랜디씨의 집에 방문했어요.
3. T 랜디 아주머니는 김씨네 가족에게 애플파이를 줬어요.

B 1. ⓑ 이 지문은 주로 김씨네 가족의 미국에서의 새로운 삶에 대한 거예요.
　ⓐ 랜디씨의 집　ⓒ 미국의 전통
2. ⓐ 김씨네 가족은 왜 랜디씨와 그의 가족에게 떡을 줬나요?
　ⓐ 이사를 하면 새로운 이웃에게 떡을 주는 것이 한국인들의 전통이기 때문에
　ⓑ 김씨네 가족이 그들에게 깜짝 선물을 주고 싶었기 때문에
　ⓒ 랜디씨와 그의 가족이 김씨네 가족을 생일파티에 초대했기 때문에
3. ⓑ '떡'은 무엇인가요?
　ⓐ 애플파이로 만든 한국 전통 음식이에요.
　ⓑ 쌀과 팥으로 만든 한국 전통 음식이에요.
　ⓒ 빵과 크림으로 만든 한국 전통 음식이에요.

C 1. immigrated 김씨네 가족은 한국에서 미국으로 이민을 왔어요.
2. take off 김씨네 가족은 신발을 벗으려 했어요.
3. exchange 이것은 훌륭한 문화 교류였어요.

Read and Understand 18쪽

1. 김씨네 가족은 이민을 왔다
2. 그녀의 새로운 이웃들에게 주기 위해
3. 그들의 옆집 이웃의 초인종을 눌렀다
4. 그리고 그들을 환영하며 안으로 맞이했다
5. 그들의 신발을 벗으려고 했다
6. 놀라운 경험　　　　7. 한국의 전통 음식인
8. 그들이 이사를 하면
9. 랜디 아주머니는 그녀에게 고마워했다
10. 훌륭한 문화 교류

Grammar Point 19쪽

1. 그것은 블록으로 만들어진 로봇이다.
2. 이것은 내 인생을 바꾼 책이다.

Workbook

A
1. 이웃
2. 인사하다
3. 환영하다
4. 벗다
5. 놀라운
6. 경험
7. 전통적인
8. 설명하다
9. 문화의
10. 교류

B
1. ⓒ
2. ⓐ
3. ⓓ
4. ⓔ
5. ⓑ
6. ⓖ
7. ⓙ
8. ⓗ
9. ⓘ
10. ⓕ

C
1. immigrated
2. neighbors
3. rang
4. welcomed
5. off
6. surprising
7. that
8. explained
9. move
10. invited
11. exchange

포카혼타스는 미국 원주민 역사에서 가장 유명한 여성들 중 한 명이에요. 존 스미스의 목숨을 구한 포카혼타스에 관한 유명한 이야기가 있어요.

포카혼타스는 포와탄 부족 추장의 딸이었어요. 그들은 미국 원주민들이었어요. 포카혼타스가 열두 살쯤이었을 때, 낯선 영국인들이 포와탄 부족을 찾아왔어요. 그들은 포와탄 부족의 땅을 빼앗고 싶어 해서 포와탄 부족과 영국인들은 싸움을 벌였어요.

어느 날, 영국인들의 지도자인 존 스미스가 잡혔고, 포와탄의 추장이 그를 막 죽이려던 참이었어요. 포카혼타스는 그녀의 아빠에게 그 남자를 죽이지 말라고 간청하여 그를 구했어요. 그녀는 그들 양쪽 모두가 평화와 조화 속에서 살기를 원했어요. 포카혼타스는 미국 원주민들과 영국인들 사이에서 중요한 역할을 했어요.

Comprehension Check   21쪽

A   1. T   포와탄 사람들은 미국 원주민이었어요.
    2. T   포카혼타스는 포와탄 부족 추장의 딸이었어요.
    3. F   포카혼타스는 포와탄의 지도자를 구했어요.

B   1. ⓐ 이 지문은 주로 포카혼타스에 대한 거예요.
       ⓑ 영국인들 ⓒ 포와탄 사람들
    2. ⓒ 포와탄의 추장은 왜 존 스미스를 죽이려 했나요?
       ⓐ 존 스미스가 포카혼타스와 결혼하고 싶어해서
       ⓑ 미국 원주민들이 영국으로 이주하길 원해서
       ⓒ 영국인들이 그들의 땅을 빼앗고 싶어해서
    3. ⓑ 누가 존 스미스를 구했나요?
       ⓐ 영국인들의 지도자 ⓑ 포카혼타스
       ⓒ 미국 원주민들

C   1. women 포카혼타스는 미국 원주민 역사에서 가장 유명한 여성들 중 한 명이에요.
    2. famous, life 존 스미스의 목숨을 구한 포카혼타스에 관한 유명한 이야기가 있어요.
    3. twelve, strange 포카혼타스가 열두 살쯤이었을 때, 낯선 영국인들이 포와탄 부족을 찾아왔어요.

Read and Understand   22쪽

1. 가장 유명한 여성들 중 한 명
2. 존 스미스의 목숨을 구한

3. 추장의 딸
4. 미국 원주민들
5. 낯선 영국인들이
6. 그들의 땅을 빼앗기를
7. 그를 막 죽이려던 참이었다
8. 그 남자를 죽이지 말라고
9. 평화와 조화 속에서 살기를
10. 포카혼타스는 중요한 역할을 했다

Grammar Point   23쪽

1. 그는 세상에서 가장 부유한 사람들 중 한 명이다.
2. 야구는 한국에서 가장 인기 있는 스포츠들 중 하나이다.

Workbook

A

1. 여자들
2. 역사
3. 추장, 족장
4. 낯선, 이상한
5. 지도자, 대표
6. 간청하다
7. 구하다
8. 평화
9. 조화
10. 역할을 하다

B

1. ⓑ
2. ⓓ
3. ⓐ
4. ⓔ
5. ⓒ
6. ⓙ
7. ⓘ
8. ⓕ
9. ⓗ
10. ⓖ

C

1. women
2. life
3. daughter
4. Americans
5. Englishmen
6. land
7. was caught
8. about
9. begged
10. rescued
11. peace
12. role

Pinocchio | 피노키오

옛날 옛날에 한 목수가 말하는 나무 토막을 발견해서 그의 친구인 제페토에게 줬어요. 제페토는 꼭두각시 인형을 만들고 싶어서 그것을 집으로 가져갔어요. 제페토는 꼭두각시 인형을 피노키오라고 부르려고 했어요.

제페토가 나무를 깎기 시작했을 때, 어떤 목소리가 꽥액 하고 소리를 질렀어요. "아야! 아프잖아!" 제페토는 나무가 살아 있다는 것을 발견하고 놀랐어요. 그는 머리, 머리카락, 눈, 그리고 코를 조각했어요. 제페토가 코를 다 깎자, 코가 점점 길어졌어요. 제페토는 코를 잘라 냈지만, 코는 기다란 상태로 남아 있었어요.

제페토가 피노키오를 거의 다 만들었을 때, 피노키오는 제페토의 가발을 벗겨서 집에서 달아났어요. "이 말썽꾸러기! 돌아와!" 제페토는 소리쳤지만, 제페토가 귀를 조각하는 것을 깜빡했기 때문에 피노키오는 들을 수가 없었어요.

Comprehension Check 25쪽

A 1. T 이상한 나무 토막은 말할 수 있었어요.
  2. F 제페토는 말썽꾸러기 소년을 만들고 싶었어요.
  3. F 제페토가 귀를 다 깎자 귀가 점점 길어졌어요.

B 1. ⓐ 이 지문은 주로 말하는 나무로 된 인형에 대한 거예요.
  ⓑ 목수 ⓒ 피노키오의 긴 코
  2. ⓐ 제페토는 무엇을 만들고 싶어했나요?
  ⓐ 꼭두각시 인형 ⓑ 장난감 로봇 ⓒ 의자
  3. ⓒ 피노키오는 왜 들을 수 없었나요?
  ⓐ 귀를 다쳤기 때문에
  ⓑ 귀가 길어졌기 때문에
  ⓒ 제페토가 귀를 조각하는 것을 잊었기 때문에

C 1. wood 옛날 옛날에 한 목수가 말하는 나무 토막을 발견했어요.
  2. carve 그가 나무를 깎기 시작했을 때, 어떤 목소리가 꽥액 하고 소리를 질렀어요.
  3. wig, away 피노키오는 제페토의 가발을 벗겨서 집에서 달아났어요.

Read and Understand 26쪽

1. 말하는 나무 토막을
2. 꼭두각시 인형을 만들기를
3. 그 꼭두각시 인형을 피노키오라고
4. 나무를 깎는 것을
5. 그 나무가 살아 있다는 것을 발견해서
7. 그것은 점점 더 길어졌다
8. 제페토가 그것을 잘라 냈다
9. 그리고 집에서 달아났다
10. 제페토가 잊었기 때문에

Grammar Point 27쪽

1. 달리고 있는 남자는 나의 삼촌이다.
2. 나는 날아다니는 로봇을 사고 싶다.

Workbook

A
1. 목수
2. 꼭두각시 인형
3. 조각하다
4. 놀란
5. 살아 있는
6. 계속[여전히] ~이다
7. 끝내다
8. 가발
9. 소리를[비명을] 지르다
10. 잊어버리다

B
1. ⓔ
2. ⓒ
3. ⓓ
4. ⓑ
5. ⓐ
6. ⓗ
7. ⓘ
8. ⓙ
9. ⓖ
10. ⓕ

C
1. talking
2. puppet
3. carve
4. squealed
5. surprised
6. alive
7. longer and longer
8. remained
9. making
10. wig
11. screamed
12. had forgotten

대부분의 사람들은 꽃을 생각할 때 달콤한 향기를 떠올려요. 하지만 항상 그렇지는 않아요. 모든 꽃이 향기로운 냄새가 나는 것은 아니에요. 사실 어떤 꽃들은 악취가 나요. 수마트라에 있는 거대한 꽃인 타이탄 아룸은 썩은 고기 같은 냄새가 나요. 꽃이 수분될 수 있도록 이 냄새는 파리를 유인해요.

꽃은 왜 향기가 날까요? 분명 이유가 있을 거예요. 꽃은 곤충이나 새를 유인하기 위해 화학 물질을 만들어요. 그들은 꽃으로 와서 수분을 시켜요.

꽃은 각각 다른 꽃가루 매개체를 유인하기 때문에 다른 냄새가 나요. 벌과 나비에 의해 수분되는 꽃은 달콤한 향기가 나요. 나방에 의해 수분되는 꽃은 낮보다 밤에 더 강한 향기가 나요. 박쥐에 의해 수분되는 꽃은 퀴퀴한 악취가 나요. 딱정벌레에 의해 수분되는 꽃은 과일 향이 나요.

Comprehension Check 29쪽

A 1. T 어떤 꽃들은 정말 안 좋은 냄새가 나요.
   2. T 타이탄 아룸은 꽃이 수분될 수 있도록 파리를 유인해요.
   3. F 꽃은 사람을 유인하는 화학물질을 만들어요.

B 1. ⓒ 이 지문은 주로 <u>꽃의 향기</u>에 대한 거예요.
     ⓐ 꽃의 크기　ⓑ 꽃의 모양
   2. ⓐ 어떤 꽃들이 퀴퀴한 악취를 가지고 있나요?
     ⓐ 박쥐들에 의해 수분되는 꽃들
     ⓑ 새들에 의해 수분되는 꽃들
     ⓒ 벌들에 의해 수분되는 꽃들
   3. ⓒ 글에 따르면 무엇이 사실인가요?
     ⓐ 모든 꽃들은 달콤한 향기가 난다.
     ⓑ 오직 새들만이 꽃들을 수분을 시킬 수 있다.
     ⓒ 타이탄 아룸은 파리에 의해 수분될 수 있어요.

C 1. fact, stink 모든 꽃이 향기로운 냄새가 나는 것은 아니에요. <u>사실</u> 어떤 꽃들은 <u>악취</u>가 나요.
   2. rotten 타이탄 아룸은 <u>썩은</u> 고기 같은 냄새가 나요.
   3. moths <u>나방</u>에 의해 수분되는 꽃은 낮보다 밤에 더 강한 향기가 나요.

Read and Understand 30쪽

1. 그들은 달콤한 향기를 떠올린다

2. 항상 그렇지는 않다
3. 향기로운[달콤한] 냄새가 난다
4. 어떤 꽃들은 악취가 난다
5. 썩은 고기 같은 냄새가 난다
6. 이 냄새는 파리들을 유인한다
8. 곤충들이나 새들을 유인하기 위해서
9. 그리고 꽃을 수분시킬 것이다
10. 다른 꽃가루 매개체를
11. 달콤한 향기가 난다
12. 나방에 의해 수분되는
13. 퀴퀴한 악취가 난다
14. 딱정벌레에 의해 수분되는

Grammar Point 31쪽

1. 피터라는 이름의 남자아이가 그 이야기를 썼다.
2. 초콜릿으로 덮인 저 케이크 좀 봐!

Workbook

A
1. 향기
2. 사실은
3. 악취가 나다
4. 썩은
5. 고기, 살
6. 유인하다
7. 수분하다
8. 화학 물질
9. 곤충
10. 악취

B
1. ⓑ
2. ⓒ
3. ⓐ
4. ⓔ
5. ⓓ
6. ⓘ
7. ⓗ
8. ⓙ
9. ⓕ
10. ⓖ

C
1. scents
2. always
3. In
4. stink
5. rotten
6. so that
7. reason
8. chemicals
9. pollinators
10. by
11. pollinated
12. odors

Exploring a Cave | 동굴 탐험하기

오늘 우리 반은 동굴을 탐험하기 위해 체험학습을 갔어요. 우리는 모두 동굴에 들어가는 것이 신이 나기도 하고 긴장되기도 했어요.

동굴에 들어갔을 때 우리는 돌 위에서 자라고 있는 이끼와 거미줄들을 봤어요. 우리가 이끼 위를 기어가는 하얀 달팽이 몇 마리를 지나갈 때, 뭔가가 우리 앞에서 팔짝 뛰어올랐어요. 모든 학생들이 비명을 질렀어요. 그것은 단지 개구리였어요. 우리는 개구리가 동굴에 산다는 것을 몰랐어요.

우리는 동굴 속으로 더 깊이 계속 걸어갔어요. 벽에서 어떤 움직임이 있었어요. 선생님이 손전등을 비추자 도마뱀이 보였어요. 그런 다음 천장에서 우리는 날개를 접고 있는 박쥐들을 봤어요. 마지막으로 동굴의 물웅덩이에서 가재를 봤어요. 우리는 동굴에 이렇게 많은 다양한 동물들이 산다는 것을 몰랐어요.

Comprehension Check 35쪽

A 1. F 학생들은 교실에서 동굴에 대해 배웠어요.
   2. T 학생들은 동굴에서 이끼와 거미줄을 봤어요.
   3. T 벽에는 움직이는 도마뱀들이 있었어요.

B 1. ⓒ 이 지문은 주로 동굴에 대한 거예요.
       ⓐ 학교 아이들 ⓑ 이끼
   2. ⓒ 학생들은 동굴에 들어가는 것에 대해 어떻게 느꼈나요?
       ⓐ 행복하고 편안하다 ⓑ 슬프고 외롭다
       ⓒ 신나고 긴장된다
   3. ⓑ 학생들이 동굴에서 본 동물이 아닌 것은?
       ⓐ 하얀 달팽이 ⓑ 이구아나 ⓒ 가재

C 1. explore 오늘 우리 반은 동굴을 탐험하기 위해 체험학습을 갔어요.
   2. deeper 우리는 동굴 속으로 더 깊이 계속 걸어갔어요.
   3. different, caves 우리는 동굴에 이렇게 많은 다양한 동물들이 산다는 것을 몰랐어요.

Read and Understand 36쪽

1. 동굴을 탐험하기 위해
2. 우리는 모두 신이 났다
3. 돌에서 자라고 있는
4. 이끼 위를 기어가고 있는
5. 모든 학생들은
6. 우리는 몰랐다
7. 우리는 계속 걸었다
8. 벽 위에서
9. 선생님이 손전등을 비췄다
10. 그들의 날개를 접고 있는
11. 물웅덩이에서
12. 그렇게 많은 다양한 동물들이 산다는 것을

Grammar Point 37쪽

1. 나는 무대 위에서 춤추고 있는 여자아이를 보았다.
2. 사람처럼 걷고 있는 저 곰을 봐.

Workbook

A
1. 탐험하다
2. 신이 난
3. 긴장한
4. 이끼
5. 달팽이
6. 기어가다
7. 팔짝 뛰다
8. 손전등
9. 천장
10. 웅덩이

B
1. ⓓ
2. ⓑ
3. ⓔ
4. ⓐ
5. ⓒ
6. ⓗ
7. ⓕ
8. ⓖ
9. ⓘ
10. ⓙ

C
1. trip
2. excited
3. growing
4. crawling
5. screamed
6. walking
7. movement
8. shone
9. ceiling
10. folding
11. Finally
12. pool

Reduce, Reuse, and Recycle | 줄이기, 재사용하기, 재활용하기

환경의 세 가지 R−줄이기, 재사용하기, 재활용하기−에 대해 알아볼 시간이에요. 매년 미국인들은 270억 개의 유리병, 3500만 톤의 음식, 6500만 개의 플라스틱과 금속 캔을 버려요. 이 모든 쓰레기는 어디로 갈까요? 그것은 모두 땅속에 남아 있다가 분해되는 데 100~4,000년이 걸려요.

환경에 도움이 되는 가장 좋은 방법은 우리가 만들어 내는 쓰레기의 양을 줄이는 거예요. 우리는 포장이 많지 않은 상품을 구입해야 해요. 환경에 도움이 되는 또 다른 방법은 물건을 버리는 대신 재사용하는 거예요. 마지막으로 기존 상품의 재료로 새로운 상품을 만들어 내도록 물건들을 재활용해야 해요. 우리는 또한 재활용된 재료를 포함한 상품을 찾아야 해요.

Comprehension Check (39쪽)

A 1. F 세 가지 R은 줄이기, 재사용하기, 돌려주기예요.
   2. T 우리는 포장이 많지 않은 상품을 구입해야 해요.
   3. F 환경에 도움이 되는 최선의 방법은 재활용하는 거예요.

B 1. ⓑ 이 지문은 주로 세 가지 R에 대한 거예요.
      ⓐ 포장 ⓒ 음식물 쓰레기
   2. ⓑ 쓰레기가 분해되는 데는 몇 년이 걸리나요?
      ⓐ 약 1년에서 50년
      ⓑ 약 100년에서 4,000년
      ⓒ 5,000년 이상
   3. ⓒ 환경을 돕는 가장 좋은 방법은 무엇인가요?
      ⓐ 포장이 많은 상품을 구입하는 것
      ⓑ 물건을 사용한 후에 버리는 것
      ⓒ 우리가 만들어내는 쓰레기의 양을 줄이는 것

C 1. environment 환경의 세 가지 R에 대해 알아볼 시간이에요.
   2. packaging 우리는 포장이 많지 않은 상품을 구입해야 해요.
   3. new, old 기존 상품의 재료로 새로운 상품을 만들어 내기 위해 물건들을 재활용해요.

Read and Understand (40쪽)

1. 알아볼 시간이다
2. 그리고 6500만 개의 플라스틱과 금속 캔을
4. 그리고 100~4,000년이 걸린다

5. 쓰레기의 양을 줄이는 것이다
6. 포장이 많지 않은
7. 그것들을 버리는 대신
8. 새로운 상품들을 만들어 내도록
9. 재활용된 재료들을 포함한

Grammar Point (41쪽)

1. 거기까지 운전하는 데 2시간이 걸린다.
2 이 방을 청소하는 데 30분이 걸린다.

Workbook

A
1. 환경
2. 줄이다
3. 재사용하다
4. 재활용하다
5. 버리다
6. 유리
7. 병
8. 100만
9. 양
10. 제품

B
1. ⓑ
2. ⓐ
3. ⓓ
4. ⓔ
5. ⓒ
6. ⓖ
7. ⓕ
8. ⓙ
9. ⓗ
10. ⓘ

C
1. learn
2. throw
3. remains
4. takes
5. way
6. reduce
7. produce
8. don't have
9. reuse
10. away
11. recycle
12. contain

Alice's Adventures in Wonderland | 이상한 나라의 앨리스

앨리스는 정원에서 자라고 있는 흰 장미들을 봤어요. 세 장의 트럼프 카드들이 분주하게 흰 장미들을 빨갛게 칠하고 있었어요. 앨리스는 이것에 대해 궁금했어요.
"흰 장미들을 왜 빨갛게 칠하는 거예요?" 앨리스가 물었어요.
"하트의 여왕은 모든 장미들이 빨간색이기를 원하셔." 스페이드 5가 대답했어요.

그때 하트의 여왕과 카드 병정들이 정원으로 왔어요. 여왕은 장미들을 확인하고는 카드 병정들에게 말했어요. "저들의 목을 베어라!" 앨리스는 화가 났어요. "안 돼요, 그럴 수는 없어요!" 앨리스가 말했어요.
"아니, 난 할 수 있어! 네 목도 벨 거야!" 여왕이 말했어요.
"안 돼, 안 돼, 안 돼!" 앨리스가 말했어요.

갑자기 앨리스의 언니가 앨리스를 깨웠어요. 앨리스는 그것이 단지 이상한 꿈이었다는 것을 깨달았어요. 그것은 이상한 나라에서의 앨리스의 모험이었어요!

Comprehension Check   43쪽

A 1. F 세 장의 트럼프 카드들이 분주하게 빨간 장미들을 하얗게 칠하고 있었어요.
2. T 하트의 여왕은 모든 장미들이 빨간색이기를 원했어요.
3. F 앨리스는 언니와 함께 이상한 나라에서 살았어요.

B 1. ⓑ 이 지문은 주로 이상한 나라에서의 앨리스의 모험에 대한 거예요.
　　ⓐ 트럼프 카드 병정들 ⓒ 하트의 여왕
2. ⓑ 앨리스는 왜 하트의 여왕에게 화가 났나요?
　　ⓐ 트럼프 카드들이 장미를 칠하는 것을 끝내지 않아서
　　ⓑ 하트의 여왕이 병정들에게 일하는 자들의 목을 베라고 명령해서
　　ⓒ 여왕이 앨리스를 잠에서 깨워서
3. ⓒ 앨리스가 하트의 여왕을 만난 후에 어떤 일이 벌어졌나요?
　　ⓐ 세 장의 트럼프 카드들이 죽었다.
　　ⓑ 앨리스와 세 장의 트럼프 카드들이 감옥에 갇혔다.
　　ⓒ 앨리스는 깨어났고 그것이 꿈이었다는 것을 깨달았다.

C 1. soldiers 하트의 여왕과 카드 병정들이 정원으로 왔어요.
2. checked, Off 여왕은 장미들을 확인하고는 카드 병정들에게 말했어요. "저들의 목을 베어라!"
3. woke 갑자기 앨리스의 언니가 앨리스를 깨웠어요.

Read and Understand   44쪽

1. 정원에서 자라고 있는
2. 분주히 칠하고 있었다
3. 앨리스는 궁금했다
4. 당신들은 왜 칠하고 있나요?
5. 모든 장미들이 빨간색이기를 원하셔
6. 정원으로 왔다
7. 여왕은 장미들을 확인했다
9. 네 목도 벨 거야
11. 앨리스를 깨웠다
12. 그것이 단지 이상한 꿈이었다는 것을
13. 그것은 앨리스의 모험이었다

Grammar Point   45쪽

1. 나는 그 방이 깨끗하기를 원한다.
2. 제인은 그녀의 방학이 끝나기를 원하지 않았다.

Workbook

A
1. 정원
2. 바쁘게
3. 칠하다
4. 여왕
5. (카드의) 하트
6. 확인하다
7. 깨웠다
8. 깨닫다
9. 모험
10. 이상한 나라

B
1. ⓒ
2. ⓔ
3. ⓐ
4. ⓑ
5. ⓓ
6. ⓙ
7. ⓕ
8. ⓖ
9. ⓘ
10. ⓗ

C
1. growing
2. busily
3. curious
4. Why
5. to be
6. Then
7. checked
8. Off
9. head
10. woke
11. realized
12. strange

A Pioneer in Tech Industry | 기술 산업의 개척자

빌 게이츠는 미국의 컴퓨터 프로그래머이자 세계에서 가장 큰 PC 소프트웨어 회사들 중 하나인 마이크로소프트의 공동 창립자예요. 그가 컴퓨터로 한 일은 전 세계에 큰 변화를 가져왔습니다.

빌은 1955년 성공한 변호사의 아들로 태어났어요. 어린 시절 빌은 똑똑하고 호기심이 많은 소년이었어요. 그는 어린 십대에 그의 첫 번째 컴퓨터 프로그램을 만들었어요. 빌은 법을 공부하기 위해 하버드 대학교에 입학했지만, 대부분의 시간을 컴퓨터를 하며 보냈어요. 1975년 그는 친구 폴 앨런과 소프트웨어 회사를 창업하기 위해 하버드 대학교를 자퇴했어요. 그 회사가 마이크로소프트였어요.

빌 게이츠는 위험을 감수하는 것을 두려워하지 않았어요. 그는 자기 자신과 그의 제품들에 자신이 있었답니다.

Comprehension Check　47쪽

A　1. T　빌 게이츠는 미국의 컴퓨터 프로그래머예요.
　　 2. F　빌은 성공한 변호사였어요.
　　 3. T　빌은 그의 친구와 소프트웨어 회사를 창업했어요.

B　1. ⓒ 이 지문은 주로 빌 게이츠에 대한 거예요.
　　　 ⓐ 마이크로소프트　ⓑ 컴퓨터 프로그램
　　 2. ⓐ 빌 게이츠를 설명하는 것이 아닌 것은?
　　　 ⓐ 유명한 변호사
　　　 ⓑ 마이크로소프트의 공동 창립자
　　　 ⓒ 컴퓨터 프로그래머
　　 3. ⓒ 빌 게이츠는 왜 하버드 대학교를 자퇴했나요?
　　　 ⓐ 그의 첫 번째 컴퓨터 프로그램을 만들기 위해서
　　　 ⓑ 돈을 벌어서 부유한 사람이 되기 위해서
　　　 ⓒ 친구와 소프트웨어 회사 마이크로소프트를 창업하기 위해서

C　1. teenager 그는 어린 십대에 그의 첫 번째 컴퓨터 프로그램을 만들었어요.
　　 2. entered, computers 빌은 법을 공부하기 위해 하버드 대학교에 입학했지만, 대부분의 시간을 컴퓨터를 하며 보냈어요.
　　 3. risks 빌 게이츠는 위험을 감수하는 것을 두려워하지 않았어요.

Read and Understand　48쪽

1. 미국의 컴퓨터 프로그래머
2. 전 세계에
3. 성공한 변호사의
4. 똑똑하고 호기심 많은 소년
5. 그의 첫 번째 컴퓨터 프로그램을
6. 하지만 그는 대부분의 시간을 보냈다
7. 그는 하버드를 자퇴했다
9. 위험을 감수하는 것을
10. 그는 자신이 있었다

Grammar Point　49쪽

1. 농구를 하고 있는 남자아이는 귀엽다.
2. 존은 이 가게의 주인인 호주 배우이다.
　（존은 이 가게의 주인이자 호주 배우이다.）

Workbook

A

1. 프로그래머	6. 썼다
2. 회사	7. 십대
3. 성공한	8. 입학하다
4. 변호사	9. (시간을) 보냈다
5. 똑똑한	10. 자신감

B

1. ⓒ	6. ⓙ
2. ⓔ	7. ⓕ
3. ⓐ	8. ⓘ
4. ⓑ	9. ⓗ
5. ⓓ	10. ⓖ

C

1. who	7. wrote
2. largest	8. entered
3. big	9. spent
4. as	10. dropped
5. successful	11. risks
6. bright	12. confidence

우리 형 케빈과 나는 뉴욕에 사는 앤 이모를 방문했어요. 이번이 우리의 첫 번째 뉴욕 방문이어서 우리는 많은 랜드마크들을 보고 싶었어요.

첫째 날에 우리는 버스를 타고 센트럴 파크에 갔어요. 센트럴 파크는 맨해튼에 위치한 공공 공원이에요. 공원은 매우 크고, 우리는 호수들, 분수들, 그리고 다리들을 봤어요.

둘째 날에 우리는 자유의 여신상을 방문하기 위해 여객선을 탔어요. 그것은 뉴욕항의 리버티 섬에 있는 거대한 조각상이에요. 우리는 엘리베이터를 타고 그 조각상의 꼭대기에 갔어요.

셋째 날에 우리는 택시를 타고 뉴욕 타임스퀘어에 갔어요. 우리는 많은 사람들과 건물들을 봤어요. 유명한 뮤지컬도 관람했어요. 우리는 앤 이모와 아주 재미있는 시간을 보냈어요.

Comprehension Check 51쪽

A **1.** F 그것은 앤 이모의 첫 번째 뉴욕 방문이었어요.
2. T 센트럴 파크는 맨해튼에 위치해 있어요.
3. F 케빈과 나는 자유의 여신상 꼭대기로 버스를 타고 갔어요.

B **1.** ⓒ 이 지문은 주로 <u>뉴욕에 방문한 것</u>에 대한 거예요.
　　ⓐ 이모 댁에 방문한 것　ⓑ 섬에 방문한 것
2. ⓒ 첫째 날에 그들은 어디로 갔나요?
　　ⓐ 자유의 여신상　ⓑ 뉴욕 타임스퀘어
　　ⓒ 센트럴 파크
3. ⓐ 케빈과 내가 타지 않은 교통수단은 무엇인가요?
　　ⓐ 지하철　ⓑ 여객선　ⓒ 택시

C **1.** located 센트럴 파크는 맨해튼에 <u>위치한</u> 공공 공원이에요.
2. Harbor 자유의 여신상은 뉴욕<u>항</u>의 리버티 섬에 있는 거대한 조각상이에요.
3. third, took 셋째 날에 우리는 택시를 <u>타고</u> 뉴욕 타임스퀘어에 갔어요.

Read and Understand 52쪽

1. 뉴욕에 사는
2. 이번이 우리의 첫 번째 방문이었다
3. 우리는 버스를 탔다

4. 맨해튼에 위치한
5. 호수들, 분수들, 그리고 다리들을
6. 자유의 여신상을 방문하기 위해
7. 그것은 거대한 조각상이다
8. 그 조각상의 꼭대기로
9. 셋째 날에
10. 많은 사람들과 건물들을
11. 유명한 뮤지컬을
12. 우리는 무척 재미있었다

Grammar Point 53쪽

1. 나는 창문을 열어 아름다운 나무들을 봤다.
2. 그는 축구 경기를 볼 것이다.

Workbook

A
1. 이모, 고모　　　　**6.** 조각상
2. 공공의　　　　　**7.** 섬
3. 거대한　　　　　**8.** 항구
4. 분수　　　　　　**9.** 세 번째의
5. 두 번째의　　　**10.** 뮤지컬

B
1. ⓔ　　　　**6.** ⓖ
2. ⓐ　　　　**7.** ⓘ
3. ⓑ　　　　**8.** ⓗ
4. ⓒ　　　　**9.** ⓙ
5. ⓓ　　　　**10.** ⓕ

C
1. who　　　　**7.** visit
2. first　　　　**8.** Harbor
3. landmarks　**9.** top
4. took　　　　**10.** third
5. which　　　**11.** saw
6. second　　**12.** watched

남극 대륙은 지구의 최남단 대륙이며, 남극이 그곳에 있어요. 남극 대륙의 대부분은 얼음으로 덮여 있고, 그곳에는 전 세계 얼음의 거의 90%가 있어요.

남극 대륙은 지구에서 가장 추운 대륙이에요. 여름의 평균 기온은 영하 27.5도이며, 겨울의 평균 기온은 영하 60도예요. 혹독한 생활 환경 때문에 사람들은 남극 대륙에서 영구적으로 거주하지 않아요. 그곳에 사는 사람들은 대부분 과학자들이에요. 그들은 날씨, 동물, 빙하, 그리고 지구의 대기를 연구해요.

남극 대륙에 사는 잘 알려진 동물들이 있어요. 고래, 펭귄, 그리고 바다표범이 그곳에 살아요. 그들은 주로 크릴새우에 의존해서, 크릴새우는 남극 대륙에서 중요한 식량 원천이에요.

Comprehension Check 57쪽

A 1. T 남극은 남극 대륙에 있어요.
2. T 전 세계 얼음의 거의 90%가 남극 대륙에 있어요.
3. F 남극 대륙의 생활 환경은 매우 좋아요.

B 1. ⓑ 이 지문은 주로 남극 대륙에 대한 거예요.
　ⓐ 남극 ⓒ 크릴새우
2. ⓐ 남극에 주로 어떤 사람들이 사나요?
　ⓐ 과학자들 ⓑ 어부들 ⓒ 사진작가들
3. ⓒ 남극에 대해 사실인 것은?
　ⓐ 지구에서 가장 뜨거운 대륙이다.
　ⓑ 거기에 북극이 있다.
　ⓒ 지구의 최남단 대륙이다.

C 1. reside 혹독한 생활 환경 때문에 사람들은 남극 대륙에서 영구적으로 거주하지 않아요.
2. coldest 남극 대륙은 지구에서 가장 추운 대륙이에요.
3. temperature 겨울의 평균 기온은 영하 60도예요.

Read and Understand 58쪽

1. 최남단 대륙
2. 얼음으로 덮여 있다
3. 가장 추운 대륙
4. 그리고 겨울의 평균 기온은
5. 혹독한 생활 환경 때문에
6. 그곳에 사는 대부분의 사람들은
7. 그리고 지구의 대기를
8. 잘 알려진 동물들이
9. 고래들, 펭귄들, 그리고 바다표범들이
10. 그들은 주로 크릴새우에 의존한다

Grammar Point 59쪽

1. 많은 학생들이 독감 때문에 학교를 결석했다.
2. 나는 장시간 비행 때문에 무척 피곤하다.

Workbook

A
1. 남극 대륙
2. 대륙
3. 거주하다
4. 혹독한
5. (생활) 환경
6. 과학자
7. (지구의) 대기
8. 잘 알려진
9. ～에 의존하다
10. 원천, 근원

B
1. ⓓ
2. ⓐ
3. ⓑ
4. ⓔ
5. ⓒ
6. ⓖ
7. ⓕ
8. ⓘ
9. ⓗ
10. ⓙ

C
1. continent
2. is found
3. is covered
4. coldest
5. temperature
6. reside
7. because of
8. who
9. well-known
10. mostly
11. on

게슬러 남작은 시민들의 충성심을 시험하고 싶어 했던 못된 총독이었어요. 이를 위해 그는 장대에 그의 모자를 걸어 놓게 했고, 지나가는 모든 사람들은 존경심을 표하기 위해 그 모자에 절을 해야만 했어요.

어느 날, 윌리엄 텔은 그의 아들 칼과 함께 그 모자를 지나갔어요. 하지만 그는 모자에 절하지 않았어요. 그는 즉시 체포됐어요. 벌로써 게슬러는 텔에게 그의 아들의 머리 위에 있는 사과에 활을 쏘라고 했어요. 텔의 아들은 나무에 등을 기댄 채 세워졌고, 그의 머리 위에는 사과 하나가 올려졌어요.

텔은 화살 두 개를 꺼내 그의 아들을 향해 한 발을 쐈어요. 화살이 사과를 관통했어요. 게슬러는 텔에게 왜 화살을 한 개 더 갖고 있는지 물었어요. 텔은 게슬러에게 만약 첫 번째 화살이 그의 아들을 죽이면, 그는 두 번째 화살을 게슬러의 심장에 쏘려고 했다고 말했어요.

Comprehension Check 61쪽

A 1. F 지나가는 모든 사람들은 총독에게 절을 해야 했어요.
2. T 윌리엄 텔은 체포됐어요.
3. T 텔의 아들은 사과를 머리 위에 올린 채 나무에 등을 기대고 세워졌어요.

B 1. ⓑ 이 지문은 주로 윌리엄 텔에 대한 거예요.
  ⓐ 게슬러 남작 ⓒ 장대에 걸린 모자
2. ⓐ 윌리엄 텔은 몇 개의 화살을 꺼냈나요?
  ⓐ 화살 두 개 ⓑ 화살 세 개 ⓒ 화살 네 개
3. ⓐ 게슬러 남작은 왜 그의 모자를 장대에 걸어 놓게 했나요?
  ⓐ 시민들의 충성심을 시험하기 위해서
  ⓑ 마을에서 가장 훌륭한 궁수를 뽑기 위해서
  ⓒ 윌리엄 텔과 그의 아들 칼을 잡기 위해서

C 1. punishment 벌로써 게슬러는 텔에게 그의 아들 머리 위에 있는 사과에 활을 쏘라고 했어요.
2. shot 텔은 화살 두 개를 꺼냈고, 그의 아들을 향해 화살 한 발을 쐈어요.
3. asked 게슬러는 텔에게 왜 화살을 한 개 더 갖고 있는지 물었어요.

Read and Understand 62쪽

1. 시민들의 충성심을
2. 그의 모자에 절을 해야 했다
3. 그의 어린 아들 칼과 함께
5. 그는 체포됐다
6. 사과에 활을 쏘라고
7. 그리고 사과가 놓여졌다
8. 텔은 화살 두 개를 꺼냈다
9. 그것은 관통했다
10. 왜 그가 또 하나의 화살을 갖고 있는지
11. 만약 첫 번째 화살이 그의 아들을 죽이면

Grammar Point 63쪽

1. 그는 그의 차가 수리되도록 했다.
2. 나는 어제 나의 셔츠가 드라이클리닝되게 했다.

Workbook

A
1. 못된
2. 충성
3. 시민, 주민
4. 막대기, 장대
5. 절하다
6. 존경심
7. 즉시
8. 체포하다
9. 벌, 형벌
10. 놓다, 두다

B
1. ⓓ
2. ⓐ
3. ⓔ
4. ⓑ
5. ⓒ
6. ⓗ
7. ⓘ
8. ⓙ
9. ⓖ
10. ⓕ

C
1. who
2. loyalty
3. hung
4. had to
5. was arrested
6. shoot
7. against
8. was put
9. shot
10. through
11. why
12. if

빨간색을 보면 어떤 기분이 드나요? 화가 나나요? 파란색은 어떤 가요? 똑똑한 느낌을 갖게 되나요? 서로 다른 색깔들은 서로 다른 감정들을 느끼게 해요. 사람들이 특정한 기분을 느끼도록 하는 데 색깔이 사용될 때 이것을 "색채 요법"이라고 불러요.

여러분은 아마 치과에 가는 것을 싫어할 거예요. 누가 좋아하겠어요? 치과 의사들은 환자들이 더 편하게 느끼도록 하기 위해 색채 요법을 사용해요. 그들은 벽을 초록색이나 노란색으로 칠할지도 몰라요. 초록색은 환자들이 침착함과 안정감을 느끼도록 해 줘요. 노란색은 환자들이 밝고 쾌활한 기분을 느끼게 도와줘요.

어떤 치료사들은 사람들이 부정적인 감정을 극복하도록 돕기 위해 색깔들을 사용해요. 그들은 환자들에게 색이 있는 빛을 비추거나, 그들의 몸을 색이 있는 실크로 감싸기도 해요. 치료사들은 환자들이 더 행복하고, 더 활기차고, 또는 더 편안하게 느끼도록 하기 위해 노력해요.

Comprehension Check   65쪽

A
1. T 다른 색깔은 다른 감정을 느끼게 해요.
2. F 환자들은 벽이 파란색일 때 쾌활한 기분을 느껴요.
3. T 어떤 치료사들은 사람들이 부정적인 감정을 극복하도록 돕기 위해 색깔들을 사용해요.

B
1. ⓑ 이 지문은 주로 색채 요법에 대한 거예요.
   ⓐ 다른 감정들 ⓒ 치과 의사들
2. ⓒ 이야기에 따르면, 어느 색이 침착함과 안정감을 느끼게 해주나요?
   ⓐ 노란색 ⓑ 파란색 ⓒ 초록색
3. ⓐ 치료사들은 어떻게 색을 사용하여 환자들을 돕나요?
   ⓐ 환자들에게 색이 있는 빛을 비춘다.
   ⓑ 벽을 빨간색으로 칠한다.
   ⓒ 환자들에게 노란색 약을 준다.

C
1. patients 치과 의사들은 환자들이 더 편하게 느끼도록 하기 위해 색채 요법을 사용해요.
2. green, yellow 치과 의사들은 벽을 초록색이나 노란색으로 칠할지도 몰라요.
3. energetic 치료사들은 환자들이 더 행복하고, 더 활기차고, 또는 더 편안하게 느끼도록 하기 위해 노력해요.

Read and Understand   66쪽

1. 당신은 어떻게 느끼는가?
2. 똑똑하다고 느끼게
3. 다른 감정들을 느끼게
4. 색깔들이 사용될 때
5. 당신은 아마 좋아하지 않을 것이다
6. 그들의 환자들이 더 편하게 느끼도록 하기 위해
7. 그들은 칠할지도 모른다
8. 침착함과 안정감을 느끼도록
9. 밝고 쾌활한 기분을 느끼도록
10. 부정적인 감정들을 극복하도록
11. 또는 그들의 몸을 감싼다
12. 더 행복하고, 더 활기차고, 또는 더 편안하게

Grammar Point   67쪽

1. 네가 준비되면 내게 알려줘.
2. 그는 스트레스를 받으면 운동을 아주 열심히 한다.

Workbook

A
1. 감정
2. 치과의사
3. 환자
4. 침착한
5. 안심하는
6. 극복하다
7. 부정적인
8. 감싸다
9. 활기찬
10. 편안한

B
1. ⓓ
2. ⓐ
3. ⓑ
4. ⓒ
5. ⓔ
6. ⓙ
7. ⓗ
8. ⓕ
9. ⓖ
10. ⓘ

C
1. when
2. smart
3. emotions
4. certain
5. therapy
6. green
7. secure
8. bright
9. therapists
10. negative
11. wrap
12. more energetic

닉은 슈퍼히어로 이야기를 읽는 것을 무척 좋아했어요. 그는 항상 슈퍼히어로로처럼 되고 싶었어요. 그는 뭔가를 할 때마다 슈퍼히어로로처럼 했어요.

닉은 엄마의 심부름을 할 때 최대한 빨리 달렸어요. 숙제를 할 때는 스톱워치로 시간을 쟀어요. 방을 청소할 때는 혼자 힘으로 모든 가구들을 옮겼어요. 자전거를 타고 학교에 갈 때는 스쿨버스와 경주를 했어요. 그는 놀이터에 가면 친구들과 놀지 않았어요. 그는 정글짐의 꼭대기에 올라가서 다른 아이들을 지켜봤어요.

닉은 언젠가 슈퍼히어로로처럼 다른 사람들을 도울 수 있을 거라고 믿었어요. 그래서 그는 항상 스스로를 단련시켰어요.

Comprehension Check　69쪽

A　1. T　닉은 항상 슈퍼히어로로처럼 되고 싶었어요.
　　2. T　닉은 엄마의 심부름을 하기 위해 최대한 빨리 달렸어요.
　　3. F　그는 자전거를 타고 학교에 갈 때 다른 자전거들과 경주를 했어요.

B　1. ⓑ 이 지문은 주로 <u>슈퍼히어로로가 되고 싶은</u> 소년에 대한 거예요.
　　　ⓐ 슈퍼히어로를 보고 있는 소년　ⓒ 강한 소년
　　2. ⓒ 닉이 숙제를 할 때 무엇을 사용했나요?
　　　ⓐ 슈퍼히어로 이야기 책　ⓑ 자전거　ⓒ 스톱워치
　　3. ⓐ 닉이 왜 항상 스스로를 단련했나요?
　　　ⓐ 언젠가 슈퍼히어로로처럼 다른 사람들을 돕기 위해
　　　ⓑ 엄마에게 좋은 인상을 주기 위해
　　　ⓒ 경주에서 이기기 위해

C　1. superhero 닉은 슈퍼히어로 이야기를 읽는 것을 무척 좋아했어요.
　　2. watch 그는 정글짐의 꼭대기에 올라가서 다른 아이들을 <u>지켜봤어요</u>.
　　3. moved, single-handedly 그는 방을 청소할 때 <u>혼자 힘으로</u> 모든 가구들을 <u>옮겼어요</u>.

Read and Understand　70쪽

1. 슈퍼히어로 이야기 읽는 것을
2. 슈퍼히어로로처럼 되는 것을
3. 그는 뭔가를 할 때마다

4. 최대한 빨리
5. 그는 스스로를 시간을 쟀다
6. 그는 그의 방을 청소할 때
7. 그는 스쿨버스와 경주를 했다
8. 그는 그의 친구들과 놀지 않았다
9. 그리고 다른 아이들을 지켜봤다
10. 언젠가 그가 다른 사람들을 도울 수 있을 거라고
11. 그는 스스로를 단련시켰다

Grammar Point　71쪽

1. 나는 우리 형과 피자를 먹을 때 최대한 빨리 먹었다.
2. 그녀는 최대한 느리게 말했다.

Workbook

A
1. 슈퍼히어로　　6. 경주하다
2. ~할 때마다　　7. 놀이터
3. 심부름　　　　8. 지켜보다
4. 스톱워치　　　9. 믿다
5. 가구　　　　　10. 훈련시키다

B
1. ⓑ　　6. ⓖ
2. ⓐ　　7. ⓕ
3. ⓓ　　8. ⓙ
4. ⓔ　　9. ⓗ
5. ⓒ　　10. ⓘ

C
1. like　　　7. furniture
2. Whenever　8. rode
3. ran　　　 9. against
4. fast　　　10. over
5. timed　　 11. others
6. cleaned　 12. trained

이집트의 피라미드처럼 스톤헨지는 세계적인 고대 미스터리예요. 스톤헨지는 매우 기이한 모습이에요. 확 트인 푸른 평야 위에 높이가 거의 9미터나 되는 거대한 직사각형 돌들이 수직으로 서 있어요. 이 돌들 위에는 다른 돌들이 놓여 있어요. 누가 그곳에 그 돌들을 놓았을까요? 그리고 이유는 무엇일까요?

우리는 정확한 이유를 절대 알지 못할 수도 있어요. 그 이유 중 하나는 700년이 넘는 시간 동안 여러 집단들이 스톤헨지를 지었기 때문이에요. 먼저 사람들은 땅에 파 놓은 원을 따라 죽은 사람들을 묻었어요. 그런 후에 사람들은 태양과 달, 별의 위치를 표시하기 위해 나무 막대기들을 동그랗게 세웠어요. 마지막으로 돌들이 동그랗게 세워졌어요. 스톤헨지는 묘지로 시작했어요. 그것은 나중에 숭배와 미스터리의 장소가 되었어요.

Comprehension Check　73쪽

A 1. T 스톤헨지는 세계적인 고대 미스터리예요.
　2. F 스톤헨지는 산꼭대기에 있어요.
　3. T 스톤헨지는 묘지로 시작했어요.

B 1. ⓒ 이 지문은 주로 스톤헨지에 대한 거예요.
　　ⓐ 이집트의 피라미드　ⓑ 돌들
　2. ⓑ 스톤헨지는 어떻게 생겼나요?
　　ⓐ 거대한 둥근 돌들이 원형으로 세워져 있고, 나무들이 주변에서 자라고 있다.
　　ⓑ 거대한 직사각형 돌들이 수직으로 세워져 있고, 돌들이 그것들 위에 놓여 있다.
　　ⓒ 나무 막대기들이 원형으로 세워져 있다.
　3. ⓒ 스톤헨지에 대해 사실이 아닌 것은?
　　ⓐ 그것은 세계적인 고대 미스터리다.
　　ⓑ 700여년 동안 여러 집단들이 지었다.
　　ⓒ 숭배의 장소로 시작해서 묘지가 되었다.

C 1. plain, upright 확 트인 푸른 평야 위에 높이가 거의 9미터나 되는 거대한 직사각형 돌들이 수직으로 서 있어요.
　2. poles, mark 그런 후에 사람들은 태양과 달, 별의 위치를 표시하기 위해 나무 막대기들을 동그랗게 세웠어요.

Read and Understand　74쪽

1. 세계적인 고대의 미스터리이다
2. 매우 기이한 모습

3. 거대한 직사각형 돌들이 수직으로 서 있다
4. 다른 돌들이 놓여져 있다
5. 누가 그 돌들을 놓았을까?
6. 우리는 절대 알지 못할 수도 있다
7. 여러 집단들이 스톤헨지를 지었다는 것
8. 그들이 땅에 파 놓은
9. 위치를 표시하기 위해서
10. 돌들이 세워졌다
11. 묘지로
12. 숭배와 미스터리의 장소가

Grammar Point　75쪽

1. 프랑스에 사는 나의 가장 친한 친구는 매우 똑똑하다.
2. 그는 집까지 내내 달려간 후, 빠르게 문을 열었고, 재빨리 닫아 버렸다.

Workbook

A
1. 고대의
2. 미스터리
3. 광경, 모습
4. 평야
5. 똑바른, 수직의
6. 묻다
7. 표시하다
8. 위치
9. 묘지
10. 숭배, 예배

B
1. ⓒ
2. ⓓ
3. ⓐ
4. ⓔ
5. ⓑ
6. ⓗ
7. ⓙ
8. ⓖ
9. ⓕ
10. ⓘ

C
1. mystery
2. sight
3. rectangular
4. placed
5. exactly
6. over
7. dead
8. dug
9. wooden
10. circle
11. graveyard
12. worship

로빈슨 크루소는 남아메리카 해안에서 조난 당했어요. 그는 거대한 폭풍우에서 살아남아 섬의 해안으로 쓸려 왔어요. 그는 자신이 난파선의 유일한 생존자라는 것을 알게 됐어요.

크루소는 살고 싶었어요. 그래서 그는 음식과 야생동물들로부터 자신을 보호할 주거지를 어떻게 마련할지 계획을 세웠어요. 그는 난파선을 뒤져서 음식과 유용한 물건들을 모았어요. 비스킷, 말린 고기, 술, 작은 망원경, 도끼, 총 몇 개를 찾았어요.

시간이 흐르는 동안 크루소는 카누와 집들 같은 유용한 것들을 많이 지었어요. 그는 또한 농사에 대해 알게 됐어요. 섬에서 약 15년을 지낸 후에 그는 사람의 발자국을 발견했어요. 섬에 살고 있는 사람들이 있었던 거예요. 그들은 누구일까요?

Comprehension Check 79쪽

A 1. T 배는 폭풍우 때문에 난파되었어요.
2. T 크루소는 난파선에서 말린 고기를 가져왔어요.
3. F 크루소는 15년 후에 섬을 떠났어요.

B 1. ⓐ 이 지문은 주로 <u>로빈슨 크루소의 생존</u>에 대한 거예요.
ⓑ 이상한 섬 ⓒ 남미의 해안
2. ⓒ 로빈손 크루소가 난파선에서 찾은 것은 무엇인가요?
ⓐ 약간의 빵 ⓑ 칼들 ⓒ 작은 망원경
3. ⓑ 해안으로 쓸려온 후 로빈손이 가장 먼저 한 일은 무엇인가요?
ⓐ 집과 같은 유용한 것들을 만들었다.
ⓑ 음식과 주거지를 어떻게 마련할지 계획했다.
ⓒ 사람 발자국을 찾았다.

C 1. survivor 크루소는 자신이 난파선의 유일한 <u>생존자</u>라는 것을 알게 됐어요.
2. fifteen, footprints 섬에서 약 <u>15년</u>을 보낸 후에 그는 사람의 <u>발자국</u>을 발견했어요.
3. living 섬에 <u>살고 있는</u> 사람들이 있었어요.

Read and Understand 80쪽

1. 로빈슨 크루소는 조난 당했다.
2. 거대한 폭풍우에서
3. 그가 유일한 생존자라는 것을
4. 야생 동물들로부터 자신을 보호할

5. 음식과 유용한 물건들을
6. 약간의 말린 고기
7. 많은 유용한 것들을
8. 농사에 대해
9. 사람의 발자국들을
10. 섬에 살고 있는

Grammar Point 81쪽

1. 나는 탁자 위에서 내 열쇠들을 찾았다.
2. 나는 두 시간 동안 내 열쇠들을 찾고 있는 중이다.

Workbook

A
1. 해안
2. 살아남다
3. 해안
4. 생존자
5. 난파선; 난파시키다
6. 주거지
7. 야생의
8. 건설하다
9. 농사
10. 발자국

B
1. ⓑ
2. ⓓ
3. ⓐ
4. ⓒ
5. ⓔ
6. ⓗ
7. ⓙ
8. ⓕ
9. ⓖ
10. ⓘ

C
1. off
2. survived
3. survivor
4. protect
5. wrecked
6. found
7. As
8. constructed
9. farming
10. spending
11. footprints
12. men

Understanding AI | AI 이해하기

AI, 또는 인공지능은 배우고 생각할 수 있는 똑똑한 컴퓨터와 같아요. 그것은 우리가 매일 보는 많은 것들에 사용돼요.

예를 들어, 당신이 시리나 알렉사에게 말을 걸 때, 그것은 당신을 도와주는 AI예요. AI는 게임을 할 수도 있고, 질문에 답할 수도 있으며, 심지어 의사들이 환자에게 어떤 문제가 있는지 찾는 것도 도와줄 수 있어요. 또한, AI는 언어를 번역해 주어서 다른 언어를 말하는 사람과 대화할 수 있게 돼요. 사람들이 일을 더 빠르고 더 잘할 수 있도록 도와주는 로봇의 뇌 같은 거라고 AI를 생각해 보세요. 학교에서는 AI가 재미있는 퀴즈와 게임을 제공해서 당신이 배우는 것을 도와줄 수 있어요.

공상 과학 소설처럼 들릴 수 있지만, AI는 실제 생활에서 우리를 돕기 위해 여기 있으며, 우리의 삶을 더 쉽고 재미있게 만들어주고 있어요.

Comprehension Check　83쪽

A　1. T　AI는 똑똑한 컴퓨터 같아요.
　　2. F　AI는 중국어를 영어로 번역할 수 없어요.
　　3. F　AI는 우리의 현실에서 찾기 어려워요.

B　1. ⓒ 이 지문은 AI가 어떻게 매일의 삶에서 사람들을 돕는지에 대한 거예요.
　　　　ⓐ 누가 AI를 만들었는지
　　　　ⓑ 어떻게 AI가 사람에게 해로울 수 있는지
　　2. ⓑ 다음 중 지문에서 AI가 이용되는 예시로 언급되지 않은 것은?
　　　　ⓐ 환자를 진찰하는 의사 도와주기
　　　　ⓑ 운전하기　ⓒ 언어 번역하기
　　3. ⓑ 지문에 따르면, AI는 어떻게 학교에서 도움을 주나요?
　　　　ⓐ 교실에서 아이들을 가르치는 것으로써
　　　　ⓑ 재미있는 퀴즈와 학습용 게임을 제공함으로써
　　　　ⓒ 모든 학생들의 숙제에 성적을 매김으로써

C　1. helping 당신이 시리나 알렉사에게 말을 걸 때, 그것은 당신을 도와주는 AI예요.
　　2. brain, faster 사람들이 일을 더 빠르고 더 잘할 수 있도록 도와주는 로봇의 뇌 같은 거라고 AI를 생각해 보세요.
　　3. real, fun AI는 실제 생활에서 우리를 돕기 위해 여기 있으며, 우리의 삶을 더 쉽고 재미있게 만들어주고 있어요.

Read and Understand　84쪽

1. 배우고 생각할 수 있는
2. 그것은 사용된다
3. 예를 들어 / 그것이 당신을 도와주는 AI이다
4. 질문에 대답할 수 있다 / 환자들에게 무엇이 잘못되었는지
5. 그것은 또한 언어를 번역할 수 있다
6. 일을 하도록 / 더 빠르고 더 잘하게
7. AI는 도울 수 있다 / 당신이 배우도록
8. 우리를 돕기 위해 / 더 쉽고 더 재미있게

Grammar Point　85쪽

1. 넬리는 매일 운동함으로써 건강하게 유지해요.
2. 케빈은 온라인 영상을 시청함으로써 요리를 배웠어요.

Workbook

A
1. 인공의
2. 지능
3. 심지어
4. 환자
5. 번역하다
6. 언어
7. 뇌
8. ～처럼 들리다
9. 공상 과학 소설
10. 현실, 실제 상황

B
1. ⓓ
2. ⓒ
3. ⓐ
4. ⓔ
5. ⓑ
6. ⓗ
7. ⓘ
8. ⓙ
9. ⓖ
10. ⓕ

C
1. or
2. every day
3. when
4. helping
5. even
6. also
7. as
8. helps
9. better
10. by
11. might
12. in

Cooking for Myself | 나 자신을 위해 요리하기

나는 라이언이고 중학생이에요. 우리 부모님은 약국을 운영하셔서 밤 늦게까지 일을 하셔야 해요. 나는 외동이기 때문에, 종종 저녁을 혼자 먹어요. 우리 부모님은 내게 피자를 주문하거나 패스트푸드점에서 햄버거를 사다 먹으라고 하셨어요. 하지만 나는 항상 저녁으로 패스트푸드 음식을 먹는 것에 질렸어요.

나는 학교에서 스스로를 위해 요리하는 것은 중요하다고 배웠어요. 그것은 비만을 예방하고 건강을 유지해 줄 수 있어요. 이것은 또한 여러분을 창의적이고 독립적으로 만들어 줄 수 있어요. 그래서 나는 나 자신을 위해 음식을 요리하기로 결심했어요. 물론 나는 가스레인지와 칼을 다룰 때 조심하겠다고 부모님에게 약속했어요.

나는 인터넷을 검색해서 간단한 요리법 몇 개를 찾았어요. 우선 가장 먼저, 나는 오믈렛을 만들 거예요. 여러분도 스스로를 위해 요리해 보는 건 어때요?

Comprehension Check 87쪽

A　1. T　라이언은 중학교에 다녀요.
　　2. T　라이언은 남자 형제나 여자 형제가 없어요.
　　3. F　라이언은 엄마에게서 요리하는 법을 배웠어요.

B. 1. ⓑ 이 지문은 주로 나 자신을 위해 요리하기에 대한 거예요.
　　　 ⓐ 부모님을 위해 요리하기　ⓒ 패스트푸드 요리하기
　　2. ⓐ 라이언이 저녁으로 요리하려는 것은 무엇인가요?
　　　 ⓐ 오믈렛　ⓑ 볶음밥　ⓒ 햄버거
　　3. ⓑ 스스로를 위해 요리하는 것의 장점은 무엇인가요?
　　　 ⓐ 침착함과 안정감을 느낄 수 있다.
　　　 ⓑ 창의적이고 독립적일 수 있다.
　　　 ⓒ 시험을 통과할 수 있다.

C. 1. run 우리 부모님은 약국을 운영하셔서 밤 늦게까지 일을 하셔야 해요.
　　2. tired, of 나는 항상 저녁으로 패스트푸드 음식을 먹는 것에 질렸어요.
　　3. searched, recipes 나는 인터넷을 검색해서 간단한 요리법 몇 개를 찾았어요.

Read and Understand 88쪽

1. 나는 중학생이다
2. 우리 부모님은 약국을 운영하신다
3. 나는 외동이기 때문에
4. 나에게 피자를 주문하라고 하셨다
5. 나는 질렸다
6. 스스로를 위해 음식을 요리하는 것은
7. 그것은 비만을 예방해 줄 수 있다
8. 창의적이고 독립적으로
9. 나 자신을 위해 요리하기로
10. 나는 우리 부모님에게 약속했다
11. 나는 인터넷을 검색했다
12. 나는 요리할 것이다
13. 너 스스로를 위해

Grammar Point 89쪽

1. 우리 선생님은 우리가 교실에서 음악을 듣게 하셨다.
2. 그녀는 그들이 후식으로 아이스크림을 먹게 했다.

Workbook

A

1. 약국
2. 혼자
3. 주문하다
4. 예방하다
5. 건강한
6. 창의적인
7. 독립적인
8. 결심하다
9. 약속하다
10. 검색하다

B

1. ⓓ
2. ⓑ
3. ⓔ
4. ⓒ
5. ⓐ
6. ⓖ
7. ⓙ
8. ⓕ
9. ⓗ
10. ⓘ

C

1. run
2. only
3. order
4. eating
5. cooking
6. prevent
7. healthy
8. creative
9. careful
10. knives
11. searched
12. cooking

연못에 떠다니는 개구리 알을 본 적이 있나요? 개구리는 한 번에 알을 4,000개까지 낳아요. 하지만 대부분의 알들은 부화하지 못해요. 어떤 알들은 다른 동물들에게 먹히고, 어떤 알들은 햇빛에 말라 버리거나 물속에서 깨질 수 있어요.

알들은 약 7일 후에 부화하고 올챙이의 생애주기가 시작돼요. 올챙이는 헤엄치며 조류를 먹기 시작해요. 부화 6주 후에 올챙이는 뒷다리와 더 긴 꼬리가 자라요. 올챙이는 작은 곤충들을 잡아먹어요.

부화 9주 후에 올챙이는 꼬리가 있는 아기 개구리처럼 보여요. 이것은 새끼 개구리 또는 어린 개구리라고 불려요. 16주에 새끼 개구리는 꼬리를 잃고 어른 개구리가 돼요.

Comprehension Check　91쪽

A　1. F　대부분의 개구리 알들은 부화해요.
　　2. T　개구리 알들은 약 7일 후에 올챙이가 돼요.
　　3. F　부화 6주 후에 올챙이는 아기 개구리처럼 보여요.

B　1. ⓒ　이 지문은 주로 개구리의 생애주기에 대한 거예요.
　　　　ⓐ 개구리 알　ⓑ 개구리의 연못
　　2. ⓐ　개구리는 한 번에 몇 개의 알을 낳나요?
　　　　ⓐ 약 4,000개　ⓑ 오직 한 개　ⓒ 약 500개
　　3. ⓑ　부화한 뒤 9주된 올챙이에 대해 사실인 것은?
　　　　ⓐ 개구리가 된다.
　　　　ⓑ 꼬리가 있는 아기 개구리처럼 보인다.
　　　　ⓒ 꼬리가 없어진다.

C　1. hind, longer　부화 6주 후에 올챙이는 뒷다리와 더 긴 꼬리가 자라요.
　　2. froglet　올챙이는 꼬리가 있는 아기 개구리처럼 보여요. 이것은 새끼 개구리 또는 어린 개구리라고 불려요.
　　3. sixteen, adult　16주에 새끼 개구리는 꼬리를 잃고 어른 개구리가 돼요.

Read and Understand　92쪽

1. 당신은 본 적이 있는가?
2. 알을 4,000개까지
3. 부화하지 않을 것이다
4. 먹힐 것이다
5. 약 7일 후에
6. 헤엄치며 조류를 먹기 시작한다
7. 부화하고 6주 후에
8. 작은 곤충들을
9. 올챙이는 아기 개구리처럼 보인다
10. 그것은 불린다
11. 새끼 개구리는 꼬리를 잃는다

Grammar Point　93쪽

1. 그 물고기는 상어에게 잡아먹힐 것이다.
2. 그 팝콘은 금방 사라질 것이다.

Workbook

A

1. (물에) 떠 있다
2. 연못
3. (알을) 낳다
4. 부화하다; 부화
5. 바싹 마르다
6. 부서지다
7. 올챙이
8. 생애주기
9. 뒷다리
10. 잃다

B

1. ⓑ
2. ⓓ
3. ⓐ
4. ⓔ
5. ⓒ
6. ⓙ
7. ⓖ
8. ⓗ
9. ⓕ
10. ⓘ

C

1. seen
2. floating
3. lay
4. hatch
5. be
6. tadpoles
7. hind
8. tiny
9. with
10. froglet
11. loses
12. adult

Hercules | 헤라클레스

헤라클레스는 반은 인간이고 반은 신이었어요. 그의 아버지 제우스는 모든 신들의 왕이었고, 그의 어머니는 인간이었어요. 하지만 헤라클레스는 성인이 될 때까지 그가 일부는 신이라는 것을 몰랐어요.

제우스의 아내 헤라는 헤라클레스를 싫어했어요. 그래서 그녀는 어린 아기 헤라클레스를 죽이기 위해 모든 종류의 방법들을 시도했어요. 그녀는 심지어 헤라클레스의 아기 침대에 큰 뱀들을 보냈어요. 하지만 힘센 아기인 헤라클레스는 그 뱀들을 으스러뜨렸어요. 시간이 지나면서 헤라클레스는 강하고 용감한 남자로 성장했어요.

네메아 땅에 있는 모든 사람들은 네메아 사자를 두려워했어요. 그 사자는 커다란 이빨과 화살에도 뚫리지 않는 단단한 가죽을 가지고 있었어요. 하지만 헤라클레스는 그 사자를 죽여서 털로 코트를 만들고 사자 머리를 투구로 썼어요. 네메아 사자는 강했지만 헤라클레스는 훨씬 더 강했던 거예요.

Comprehension Check 95쪽

A 1. T 헤라클레스는 모든 신들의 왕인 제우스의 아들이었어요.
   2. F 헤라클레스의 어머니는 여신이었어요.
   3. T 헤라클레스는 강하고 용감한 남자로 성장했어요.

B 1. ⓐ 이 지문은 주로 헤라클레스에 대한 거예요.
       ⓑ 제우스 ⓒ 네메아 사자
   2. ⓑ 헤라클레스는 네메아 사자를 죽인 다음 무엇을 했나요?
       ⓐ 칼과 방패를 만들었다.
       ⓑ 코트와 투구를 만들었다.
       ⓒ 옷과 신발을 만들었다.
   3. ⓐ 헤라클레스에 대해 사실인 것은?
       ⓐ 그는 헤라가 그를 죽이기 위해 보낸 큰 뱀들을 으스러뜨렸다.
       ⓑ 그는 약한 남자로 성장했다.
       ⓒ 그의 아버지는 인간이었고 어머니는 여신이었다.

C 1. god, grown 헤라클레스는 성인이 될 때까지 그가 일부는 신이라는 것을 몰랐어요.
   2. ways, kill 헤라는 어린 아기 헤라클레스를 죽이기 위해 모든 종류의 방법들을 시도했어요.
   3. tough, pierced 네메아 사자는 커다란 이빨과 화살에도 뚫리지 않는 단단한 가죽을 가지고 있었어요.

Read and Understand 96쪽

1. 반은 인간이고 반은 신
2. 모든 신들의 왕이었다
3. 그가 성인이 될 때까지
4. 그래서 그녀는 모든 종류의 방법들을 시도했다
5. 그녀는 심지어 큰 뱀들을 보냈다
6. 그 뱀들을 으스러뜨렸다
7. 시간이 지나면서   8. 네메아 사자를 두려워했다
9. 화살에도 뚫릴 수 없는   10. 그것의 털로 코트를 만들었다
11. 하지만 헤라클레스는 훨씬 더 강했다

Grammar Point 97쪽

1. 그 괴물은 죽일 수 없었다.
2. 그는 그 성이 파괴될 수 없다고 말했다.

Workbook

A
1. 절반의
2. 다 큰, 성장한
3. 보냈다
4. 아기 침대
5. 으스러뜨리다
6. 용감한
7. 뚫다
8. (동물의) 털
9. 입었다
10. 헬멧, 투구

B
1. ⓒ
2. ⓓ
3. ⓑ
4. ⓔ
5. ⓐ
6. ⓖ
7. ⓕ
8. ⓙ
9. ⓘ
10. ⓗ

C
1. god
2. human
3. grown
4. kinds
5. sent
6. crushed
7. grew
8. of
9. be
10. out of
11. wore
12. stronger

| **Boost Up!** 1 | 32쪽 |

A 1. 숨겨진 보물을 발견해서
   2. 음악을 들어서
   3. 예상하지 못한 뉴스를 들어서

B 1. She was excited to meet her favorite singer.
   2. They were happy to win the game.

| **Boost Up!** 2 | 33쪽 |

A 1. 내가 숙제를 끝낼 수 있도록
   2. 그가 건강을 유지하기 위해서
   3. 저녁식사 할 준비가 되도록

B 1. She sets an alarm so that she wakes up on time.
   2. I sent the package yesterday so that it would
      arrive early.

| **Boost Up!** 3 | 54쪽 |

A 1. 화창한 날을 즐기는
   2. 새로운 것을 배우는
   3. 친구를 사귀는

B 1. A good way to reduce stress is to listen to
      music.
   2. A fun way to express feelings is to draw pictures.

| **Boost Up!** 4 | 55쪽 |

A 1. 정원에서 피고 있는
   2. 하늘을 날고 있는
   3. 공원에서 놀고 있는

B 1. We saw the leaves falling from the trees.
   2. They saw a rainbow appearing after the rain.

| **Boost Up!** 5 | 76쪽 |

A 1. 가장 똑똑한 학생
   2. 가장 빠른 주자
   3. 가장 맑은 호수

B 1. He is the most talented singer in the competition.
   2. This is the most beautiful place in the world.

| **Boost Up!** 6 | 77쪽 |

A 1. 우리는 회의에 참석하고 싶다
   2. 그가 차를 조심스럽게 운전했다
   3. 아버지가 더 많은 돈을 절약했다

B 1. This is why they repaired the bike before the trip.
   2. This is why I decided to help my neighbor
      every weekend.

| **Boost Up!** 7 | 98쪽 |

A 1. 배우도록
   2. 그녀가 늘 하고 싶어했던 것을
   3. 저녁으로 무엇을 먹을지

B 1. I helped my friend choose what she'll wear for
      the party.
   2. The police officer asked her to explain what she
      saw last night.

| **Boost Up!** 8 | 99쪽 |

A 1. 새로운 취미를 시작해 보는 게
   2. 파티에 가는 게
   3. 너의 목표에 집중하는 게

B 1. Why don't you read a book before going to
      bed?
   2. Why don't you attend the event after school?

기적의 직독직해 120 words B